MY LIFE AFTER AUSCHWITZ

(A Link in the Chain)

Eugene Heimler

Copyright © Eugene Heimler 1962

First published as *A Link in the Chain*
The Bodley Head Ltd.
London, Great Britain

Second Printing 1980
University Printing Services for
The University of Calgary
Calgary, Alberta, Canada

© The Literary Trust of Eugene Heimler 1991
Trustee: Miriam B. Heimler
For more information contact:
mheimler1@gmail.com

Cover photo: Depositphotos_1 1578930_1-2015
Cover design: Devorah Priampolsky

ISBN 978-0998959351

All rights reserved. No part of this publication may be translated, reproduced, stored in a retrieval system, or transmitted in any form or by means, electronic, mechanical, photocopying, recording, or otherwise, without prior permission in writing from both the copyright holder and the publisher.

Published and distributed by:
Miriam B. Heimler (Trustee)
The Literary Trust of Eugene Heimler
P.O.B. 18422
Jerusalem 91183
Israel

To my patients and colleagues
Without whom this book would not
have been written

Other Books by Eugene Heimler

NIGHT OF THE MIST

RESISTANCE AGAINST TYRANNY

MENTAL ILLNESS AND SOCIAL WORK

SURVIVAL IN SOCIETY
(CONSTRUCTIVE USE OF DESTRUCTIVE FORCES)

THE HEALING ECHO

THE STORM

MESSAGES: A SURVIVOR'S LETTER TO A YOUNG GERMAN

"…My son, give, I pray thee glory to the Lord, the God of Israel, and make a confession unto Him and tell me now what thou hast done; hide it not from me …"

—*The Mishna, Sanhedrin*: 6-2

'No man is an Island, entire of itself; every man is a piece of the Continent, a part of the main.'

—*John Donne, Devotions, XVII*

CONTENTS

Foreword

Book One
Part I: Arrival
Part II: Green Grass and Fog

Book Two
No Man Is an Island

Epilogue

FOREWORD

I returned to my native country, Hungary, in the summer of 1945 from the concentration camps of Germany. The experiences of that fateful year were published in my first book, *Night of the Mist,* in 1959.

I returned alone; the rest of my family had been consumed in the gas chambers of Auschwitz. I was twenty-three years old at the time and already a widower, for my young bride Eva had also found her death behind the electrified wire.

I was broken in body and spirit, and the poems that I wrote in those days spoke only of death: "... *I died in others; can I in others be born again?*"

Hungary was in ruins in more senses than one. The poisonous snakes of anti-Semitism still crawled among those ruins, and I soon had to recognize that as a Jew I was not wanted in the land in which my ancestors had lived and died for many centuries. I married again, tore up my roots and brought my tortured body and mind to England. In time I was born again in others, and today I live my life in others: in my family, in my friends, in my patients and in England.

This book is the story of that death and resurrection. Although it is a true story of my life, my conflicts and my small contribution to my adopted country, my aim is more than just to speak about the life of one insignificant man. I shall attempt in these pages to convey my belief that defeat in life can be turned into victory, provided a man, however insignificant himself, can become a part of something greater: humanity and other human beings.

It is this belonging to the whole that makes my life meaningful today; this is the foundation of my newly found faith. And it is this that gives me the strength to speak as frankly and unashamedly as possible.

– Westminster, March 1962

ACKNOWLEDGEMENTS

I would like to thank "Frank Latham," his wife "Evelyn," and "Joan" for their permission to use the material contained in this book and also for their warm letters encouraging me to publish it.

I am also grateful to Mr. R. Bradfield, Mrs. E. E. Irvine and Dr. G. Wigley for allowing me to use their names, and for their consent to the publication of our conversations and discussions. I am also indebted to my psychoanalyst for her permission to use the material of my analysis.

My thanks also go to Martin and Ruth Gelband, who welcomed me into their home during the summer of 1961. There I was able to spend several weeks writing this book undisturbed which would have been quite impossible in my own home while my children were enjoying their holidays!

I would also like to express my gratitude to the Middlesex County Council for the special leave granted to me to complete my book.

While the names of my patients and some other persons are fictitious, and certain circumstances in the narrative have been altered so that none of these persons are recognizable, this is a true story. Any similarity to fiction is purely coincidental. – EH

BOOK ONE

PART I: ARRIVAL

MY LIFE AFTER AUSCHWITZ

CHAPTER ONE

In the beginning, it was as though I were in a daze. My eyes saw, my ears heard, but everything passed through a strange filter of emotion that distorted and modified my world. The reality of danger was giving way to a state of misty elation that alternated with chaotic depression from hour to hour. It was May, and I was on my way home to Hungary from the concentration camps of Germany, but it almost seemed as though this fateful journey were being undertaken by someone else.

From Prague to Bratislava I traveled on a buffer of the train. My traveling companion on the other buffer was a young SS man, who at any minute could easily have pushed me off. That he was a member of the SS. I realized when he left his knapsack for a few minutes at the station and I saw his name and SS insignia smeared on the back. He wore civilian clothes and I was the only one aware of his identity. At Bratislava I bade him farewell: I was ill with jaundice and could not travel farther. He had the insolence to wish me a speedy recovery, and I was stupid enough to thank him. Then I walked towards the city as if in a dream.

A Russian patrol behind a machine gun stopped me, demanding to know where I came from. The word Buchenwald faintly registered in them the name of a German town, and they cursed me for a Fascist swine. This was so funny that an attack of laughter seized me. The Russians thought that I was laughing at them and moved nearer threateningly. Behind the fog of my insanity I was still able to comprehend that any moment I might be shot, yet I could not stop laughing. Suddenly an officer of the Red Army appeared and, inspecting

MY LIFE AFTER AUSCHWITZ

me as if I was an insect under a microscope, asked me in Yiddish, "Are you a Jew?" In the meantime another patrol had brought in some "real" Fascists, and when I saw them standing in front of the machine-guns I thought the whole scene so ridiculous that I burst out laughing again. At last the Red Army officer turned to the sergeant and said in Yiddish: "He is crazy." They let me pass, and as I left them I was still laughing. I laughed until the pain on my right side became unbearable.

Now the fog is thicker. It is a stranger who drags his thin, sick body through the strange town where people speak in an unknown tongue. Someone says: "You had better go to the offices of the JOINT." And there a woman says: "Herr Krepplach will take you to St. Elizabeth." Burning with fever, I think of Napoleon, mistaking the good saint's name for St. Helena. A Hungarian girl feels pity for me. Her name is Kato. She is young, blue-eyed and has a swollen leg, and she accompanies me to the hospital, saying to Herr Krepplach on the way: "The poor boy is out of his mind." There are many beds in the ward, and the middle-aged woman doctor asks me in Hungarian to undress. "What are these marks on your back?" "I was whipped," I reply, and feel like cuddling up to her and laying my head on her large bosom. She says to a nun: "But he is only a child." I am twenty-three.

On the wall opposite are white circles that run into each other. It is an endless chase. Beyond the circles there is a whirlpool sucking down all the colors of the sun, and beyond the whirlpool are words, father's words, mother's words and voices of unknown people from the depths of a distant past. "Rabbi, am I going to die?" The circles stand still and there is silence.

The Rabbi sitting on my bed reassures me. "You are young, my son. You will live." He asks me whether I want to return to Hungary. Would I not rather go to Palestine? "God has kept His word. There is to be a Jewish state, and from all corners of the world He will gather together His people." Or would I like to go to England? Perhaps America? The world is open now.

That night my temperature drops and I have a dream of the big chestnut trees of our garden and mother sitting in the grass. She beckons to me: "Come home, Jancsi."

No more circles, no more whirlpools, no more voices, but only tears. Mother is dead, and so is father, and Susan my sister and her child Gabi who was taken into the gas chambers at the age of two and a half. My uncles are dead, my cousins are dead, my wife is dead.

I am able now to comprehend that this is the present and yesterday is the past, and yet that the past lives on in the present, and the future lives in the present and in the past also. Kato holds my hand and says that she will wait until I am better to leave and we shall go together ... home ...

At the beginning of June 1945 the fog disappeared. The strangely colored spectacles through which I had viewed the world were also gone. The present was present now and loaded with emptiness.

One bright morning we mounted a truck making for Komarom, a town with the only remaining bridge connecting Czechoslovakia with Hungary. The rest of the bridges had been blown up by the Nazis. Halfway there the truck broke down and we had to walk towards the Danube. Kato was warm and sweet and talked of hope of a new life, of home, of how she would wait until her own people returned and then would go to Palestine. Perhaps I would join her on that journey too. As her right leg was still badly swollen our journey was slow, for I also could only just manage to drag myself along.

Suddenly, soldiers appeared on the road, running towards us. Then everything happened so suddenly that I could not comprehend for some minutes what had taken place. The soldiers dragged Kato to the roadside and raped her in front of my eyes, while others aimed their machine guns at me. Four Russians forced themselves on her within the space of a few minutes, and then they disappeared. She lay there on the ground and cried and I stood looking at her uncovered body with a storm of anger growing in me. I was angry with *her,* for reasons I did not understand. Then I started to run, but I was so weak that I fell down.

Kato lifted her head from the dust. "Jancsi ... don't ... don't leave me here." I sat by the roadside waiting for her to join me, but she just lay there as if dead. No one else was in sight. I went back and helped her to stand. She was sobbing like a child. She could not speak; and neither could I. We walked without a word towards the river.

* * *

The first sight that caught my eyes on Hungarian soil was the white paint on the walls: "DEATH TO FASCISM. DEATH TO THE GERMAN MURDERERS." Behind the fresh paint were the old, now hardly visible words: "DEATH TO JUDEO-BOLSHEVISM. DEATH TO THE JEWS." Did the same hands paint both these slogans of death on the small houses of Komarom?

At the station Kato rushed to the toilet and I went to the stationmaster's office. No regular trains to Budapest. No buses either. Goods trains? Yes, but no guarantee how long the journey will take. No tickets. On the roofs of trains or on buffers. At your own risk.

Kato emerged from the toilet with a big chunk of bread and sausages. "People have changed," she said. "They have become kind." She looked affectionately at her acquisitions. We climbed up on the roof of a cattle truck and made ourselves as comfortable as possible. She shared her food with me and we ate without a word until the train began to move. In Germany I had dreamt often about my homecoming, but I had never imagined that I would be sitting on top of a train. When I had tried to picture my first hours at home, I had always visualized a stormy sky above, and a feeling of something very dramatic. Now there wasn't even a single cloud above, and I felt nothing at all.

Suddenly Kato started to cry again. She put her head on my lap and her body trembled. I sat there motionless, and it was as if the wheels were saying: "Dirty bitch, dirty bitch."

"They would have killed me," she said, looking at me with tear-stained eyes.

"Probably."

"They would have killed you too." I felt anger rising in me again.

"So you obliged them for my sake? How nice of you!" With a desperate "Oh!" she fell on my lap and wept again. A sadistic urge made me say things that I regretted later.

"If I had wanted you, you would of course have protested in the gentle manner of your gentle sex. 'Oh no, Jancsi, we mustn't. It's wrong. It's immoral....' But to them, without a word, without a protest, you opened your legs...."

She moved away from me. I hit harder.

"I shall never forget it as long as I live, you making love to those brutes...."

She was screaming at me by now. "If you say one more word I shall throw myself off this train, so help me God!" Her eyes protruded with hate. "You coward, you bastard, you stood there watching what happened without trying to save me. You're not a man, you're an animal!"

Now quite suddenly I began to feel guilty. Not for not helping her, but for something I didn't quite understand. I felt as if *I* had done this dreadful thing to her. My bitterness gave way to pity and I moved my hands towards her. But she pushed them away. "Don't you touch me, you brute, you murderer."

"Murderer?" I asked in alarm. "Why murderer?"

The train raced towards the evening sun and the scent of the fields was rich in my nostrils. I looked at the land with new eyes. The fields were beautiful, the cows were beautiful, the little white cottages that rushed by were all miraculously beautiful. Life was good and it was good to live, and it was good to be grateful.

"I am sorry, forgive my brutality." Kato did not reply. I went on: "Forgive me. Of course none of us could have done anything. I haven't been with a woman for a long time, and those beasts awoke the beast in me too. I'm ashamed of myself."

She still turned away from me and did not reply, but there was a difference in her silence now and she stopped crying. Slowly evening fell and a chilly wind blew from the north. She sat up.

"Are you cold?" she asked, and when I replied that I was she drew nearer to me and I felt the warmth of her body. For a few moments we were at peace.

The train stopped, jerked, moved, stopped again and slowly time dissolved as the quickening rhythm of our blood threatened to overwhelm our new-found peace.

"Do you still want it?" I thought she was asking me whether I still wanted food, but she was referring to another kind of hunger. As the meaning of her words penetrated my mind the tide of desire flooded through me. I felt her body beneath her shabby clothes, and held her tiny breasts as if they were the first fruits of the year; her lips were warm, and when I kissed her I tasted her salty tears on my tongue. Then suddenly she tore herself away from me, screaming.

"They may have infected me! What if I am pregnant?"

A cold chill ran down my spine, and the tide of desire ebbed swiftly. But I continued to hold her, though without feeling, until she fell asleep. The train raced on, the engine puffing like a fat man running upstairs, while I watched the night and remembered the flames of the crematorium. At the outskirts of Budapest the train stopped again as the first light of dawn appeared on the sky. Kato turned to me.

"I could have loved you, you know that. But I can't." She stood up and climbed off the train. It was no use begging her to stay. "I don't want to face you in the daylight," she said, and disappeared into the crowd. I followed her with my eyes as long as I could. I have never seen her again.

I was lying in the garden, amid the flowers of summer, in the lush, caressing grass. For several days I had been coming here every afternoon to gaze at the window of the veranda where, once upon a time, Mother had hung out the washing. In the evening she used to come to this window, calling out, "Come, my son, supper is ready." Now behind the glass panes of the veranda strangers were living, strangers were hanging out their washing on the line – yet still I waited to see my Mother's face appear in the brown window frame.

Weeds had overrun the garden; it had been neglected for years. The summerhouse stood bare. Only the chestnut trees, swaying in the wind, were as of old. It was here that I had learnt to walk, here that I had fallen down for the first time. Here, in this garden, I searched for the past. Each pebble had a meaning, every leaf on the shrubs belonged to me, to my past, to the life of my family which had been scattered by the storm.

Beyond the gate – the town. My God, how it had changed; even the color of the houses was different. The town had died just as the people had died – and those who remained were dragging themselves through life, confused by the sense of guilt which they carried in their souls. From this once populous little town they had carried away six thousand human beings, of whom only a score had returned.

Not only this town, but my whole country seemed to have died. As I made my way homeward, everywhere I had seen burnt villages, devastated cities, unfriendly and disillusioned people. A short time before, the propaganda of ultimate victory was still being loudly declaimed; now everyone walked stealthily, not knowing when the hand of retribution would reach him.

As I lay there in the garden, all this seemed only a bad dream. "Up there on the veranda ... soon it will be evening and I shall go up and have supper with my family...." But I could not go on playing this game for long: at any moment the concierge might come out of his basement flat – a new man, who knew nothing of the former days.

Yes, it was time for me to wake up to the truth, to life, to reality. I must face the unbelievable fact that my family was no longer alive. A holocaust had obliterated us, our town, the whole country. Of all my people I alone had come back from the jaws of death.

"And now, what will happen to me? I have nobody. I have come back from the hell of hells – why should I collapse now? Or shall I kill myself...?"

No. There were others whom I had to see, messages I had to deliver to the living from the dead. There were things I had to do, words I had to utter to show the world what I had learned and lived through, on behalf of the millions who had seen it also but could no longer speak. Of their dead, burnt bodies I would be the voice.

I threaded my way along the bank of a small stream towards the flat in which I had rented a room. "I must find new clothes in place of these torn rags. I must work. I am hungry – I'll have something to eat. I must start everything from scratch. I must make something of my freedom...." And I began to walk back through the dead streets, back towards life.

MY LIFE AFTER AUSCHWITZ

CHAPTER TWO

The town where I began life for the second time is called Szombathely. The Romans named it Savaria. It was an important city in those days, as it lay on the Via Aurelia, the main road between Rome and Germany. Emperors, consuls, soldiers of Imperial Rome and also slaves marched along this road towards the mountains of the Balkans and to Rome. Apart from men of war, sculptors, architects, painters and poets lived and worked here under the shadow of the Basilica, offering their souls to Jupiter at sundown. Indeed, the majesty and glory of Rome left its mark on this part of Hungary more forcibly than elsewhere. In the 1930s educated men, particularly in the legal profession, could still speak Latin; and in an age of feudalism, discrimination and injustice the motto here remained *Fiat justizia et pereat mundus* (There shall be justice even if the world has to perish).

Many gifted Hungarian poets of this century were born here. It seemed as if there was something in the atmosphere that brought out the best in creative man. With a population of only 30,000 people, the town had two daily papers and innumerable weeklies and literary periodicals, and for a long time the Mayor of the city was a poet himself.

But the spirit of Rome was not only manifested in literature. Savaria produced singers of fame, musicians, conductors, and also lawyers who argued the word of the Roman Law and the meaning of Justice. However much the law may have been distorted at the Supreme Court in Budapest, in Savaria every man was equal before it. While the elections were open to inspection in the rest of the country, here they were conducted by secret ballot; and it was possible for my father, a Socialist, to be elected on several successive occasions as Councillor and Alderman. I was never made aware in my formative years that because of my Jewish origin my place in this country was questioned by anyone. My ancestors lived and died in this neighborhood and my family, as my father once said, had become "an historical monument." Foreigners were tolerated and many Russian prisoners of the First World War settled down to useful work and family life, treated no differently from the rest. In 1918 there was a revolution here as in other parts of the land, but no executions ever took place. When the revolution failed my father would have been hanged a few miles from here for having taken part in the Red revolt; instead he was tried and completely rehabilitated "as a man who followed his beliefs but did not allow any atrocities to occur."

It was only after 1938, when Germany occupied Austria, that the beginning of a change came, that altered Savaria's old spirit. This last stronghold of the Hungarian west that had fought and bled on the barricades of Christianity was now slowly crucified on the Arrow Cross. What Mongols and Turks had failed to achieve in past centuries, the Germans now did. They not only killed men, but killed the spirit of freedom. As the darkness grew from the west the poets stopped their rhyming and went away, never to return. Many men looked across Germany and beyond it towards the Seine and the Thames and the Hudson River, and they too left. And yet until the final hour some sanity was maintained inside the ancient walls; there were still men who spoke out unafraid against the tyranny of dictators.

During the last days of the war the Hungarian pocket Hitler set up the nation's capital in Savaria, and twenty-four hours before the Red Army took the city he declared that "this old bastion of Rome will never surrender." But this is where his story ends and mine begins, with the march of the Red Army along the Via Aurelia.

*   *   *

When I returned home, Savaria as I had known it was no more. Most of the buildings still stood there unharmed, with their memories of a glorious past preserved in the museums under lock and key. But the spirit of Rome lay dead with the ruins of the Basilica. On County Hall the Red Flag swelled proudly in the wind, a sign that the labor pains of a new age had begun. These soldiers who had fought their way across the plains of Russia and the Ukraine and across the Carpathian Mountains, bringing with them the storm of a new world, had two faces – the man and the beast. They would go out of their way to play with children, lifting them into their arms with gifts of chocolates and sweets, taking them on a pleasure cruise in their heavy tanks. Yet these men would rape the mothers and sisters of these children the same night.

At night they would sing, and the wind would carry the songs from their barracks to the town. There was beauty, tragedy, strength, power and love in these melodies; images of the endless steppes, vast mountains and powerful rivers were projected in their rhythms. The Germans here had never sung songs of life, raised their hearts never to love but always to hate. Primitive and crude as many of these Russians were, yet they were human beings like me. I could never hate the Russians, even if I learned in time to fear their politics.

As my father had died a martyr's death for his belief in a better world, and as many believed that the very world he had died for was in the making now, I was received with open arms by his former friends and comrades. Had I wanted then, at the age of twenty-three, to become a Member of Parliament, the Mayor of our town, or a diplomat, it would not have been impossible. But I wanted only one thing: to write.

Writing is not just a mechanical process; it is not merely putting down one's thoughts on paper, it is an attempt to stand naked before the world. The true writer must be willing never to conceal his anatomy from watching eyes – and no cripple likes to display his distorted body to others. Writing reveals the wounds of the soul, but it is only the mature man who is able to show his wounds without flinching.

I wanted to be a writer – but I was still full of imperfection. That year in Germany had nearly succeeded in molding me into a monster: the hate directed against me had opened up hate within me, revealing black tunnels of my mind of whose existence I had not known before. Ugly beasts of destruction now crawled in their hundreds in those tunnels, and only a small candle of faith could light my way.

It was now, with a pen in my hand, that I realized how far the Gestapo had almost succeeded in destroying the man in me; and when my words appeared in print, releasing the atmosphere of the crematorium, the smell of burnt flesh and of gas, I expressed a hate that could only destroy *me* in the end. If I had had my way then I would have been prepared to annihilate Germany, and everything in it. My articles that were printed at the time were not expressed in the words of my people, of the ancestors who had submitted to the pains of centuries and yet believed in the goodness of man. They were the words of my enemies, redirected back at them. The small candle light had not proved powerful enough to express the eternal light of the sun.

One night in the silence the memory of my father spoke across the gulf of time, and I heard his voice in the voice of the wind that was shaking the trees in front of my window. It was as though he were saying: "Is this the world that I died for, my son?" My world of hate collapsed into tears as I replied: "Forgive me, father, I was in pain."

MY LIFE AFTER AUSCHWITZ

It was an age-long night, but by dawn the tears had washed away my hate – for the time being, anyway.

Like myself, Hungary had suffered many blows, and she too was bleeding from her wounds. Like myself, too, she was about to stand up once more and breathe in the air of life and freedom. The Germans had left nothing behind them but ruins, death and bitterness. The contempt and hate of the *Herrenvolk* in the final hour had turned from the Jews and vented itself on the Hungarians, who suddenly for the first time saw the unmasked face of the Master Race. In an outburst of desperate fury, bridges had been blasted into the rivers and valuables stripped from tiny houses, results of a lifetime's work. The Hungarian Nazis had fled, followed by their faithful supporters while the rest of Hungary stood still and waited for the storm to pass. The Red Army had heroically fought its way across the Danube, closing in from every direction, until one morning in the spring of 1945 the country was occupied, and with this occupation National Socialism had reached its end.

This tiny, unfortunate land in the arms of four rivers, kneeling in front of her majestic mountains, now trembled under the boots of the Red Army. They had freed the country from an insane dictatorship, but did these liberators bring freedom or a new form of slavery from their distant land? With freedom this beautiful country could easily have become a real paradise. Her climate was healthy with seasons clearly defined, the fertile land beyond the cities eternally alive with rich soil. Life had always throbbed with a passionate rhythm in Hungary. But instead of a paradise it had become a living hell under the constant yoke of foreign occupations.

Since the day Pope Sylvester II had sent St. Stephan, the first King of Hungary, the Holy Crown, and the country had become Christian, she had fought and bled on the barricades of Christianity. First came the Germans, then the Mongols under the leadership of Genghis Khan, then the Turks, then the Germans again and yet again. A few years of breathing space; a few years of freedom – and always more oppression, rape and murder.

I was a son of this tragic land; a bitter and desperate son during those summer months, hopelessly waiting for the return of some member of my family who would help me to build a bridge that would connect me with my past. But I waited in vain; they had all been devoured by the gas chambers of Auschwitz. I despised this spineless, Hitler-worshipping mob, for which Christianity had become a weapon of hate, who watched without a word of protest the deportation of their fellow citizens to an alien land, who believed that the answer to all their problems would automatically come with our destruction. Yet I could not help but love Hungary, and felt that her destiny would also be mine. That is why the British General election on July 26 seemed so very important to me and to those few who also cared. We believed that it would have a great influence on our own free elections in the autumn. The issue at stake, however, was greater than Hungary. I sensed that perhaps the future of Europe was to be decided by the people of Britain that night. The first Atom Bomb had not yet exploded in Hiroshima but already we could feel the tremor in our hearts.

The night of the British general election we journalists of the *Free County News* took turns in our office to await developments. As the returns came in over the BBC, we drank coffee, smoked, played chess and cards, and of course talked. Most of us belonged to different parties, but one thing was certain: no former Nazi was amongst us that night. After midnight the conversation began to liven up.

Jozsi claimed that even if the Labour Party won the election, the split between East and West was unavoidable, because British Labour, not being a Marxist Party, would continue to carry out the imperialistic policy of the Conservatives. The only hope for mankind, he averred, lay in the Communist Party of the Soviet Union, and the only force capable of maintaining peace in Hungary was the Red Army. Gergely, a middle-aged journalist with graying hair and thick spectacles, pulled a face.

"My dear Jozsi," he said, "it seems to me that you can only see things in black and white, or may I say red and white? Why should the British Labour Party carry out an imperialistic policy? Why does a labor movement have to be Marxist? Whilst, agreed, Socialism in Britain may be a slow process, I think it will come in time. In any case, the age of Western Imperialism has come to an end. I wish I were so sure about the Eastern one."

Jozsi was becoming excited.

"Are you trying to insinuate that Russia is imperialistic? Is that what you mean?"

Gergely cleaned his glasses with slow deliberate movements, and when he had finished he carefully folded his handkerchief and replaced it in his coat pocket.

"I did not say that Russia was imperialistic. I merely said 'I wish I were so sure.' That's all I said."

"How can a Socialist country be imperialistic? Forgive me, but you are talking nonsense."

"I did not say that Russia was Socialist, either," said Gergely calmly.

"What is she then? Fascist?"

"To my knowledge," said Gergely quietly, "the Soviet Union is the proud bearer of Communism. Now, in my opinion there is a vast difference between the two. Socialism has its roots in democracy, Communism has not. You never know what a dictator may do. Today he may do one thing, tomorrow just the opposite."

Jozsi went red in the face and the peaceful conversation might have taken a violent turn had we not been interrupted by the first result. Soon it became clear that Labour had a sweeping victory. With the exception of Jozsi and Janos, an ardent Roman Catholic, we were all pleased with the results.

"Immature nation, a Godless lot, the British," muttered Janos bitterly; "bringing the Reds in. But then, what can we expect from Protestants anyway?"

I flared up. "You dare to say that *they* are immature? You speak of God? Where were you and your God-fearing churchgoers in the last few years? Over there, with those who fought against Satan, or over here with those who fought beside him?"

He answered slowly and thoughtfully: "As far as I am concerned Satan at the moment is still out there," and he pointed towards the streets. "Only this time he wears another uniform."

"I don't like occupation by any country," said Gergely, and yawned. "But so far the Russians have behaved quite decently."

"Decent?" Janos hissed the words. "You dare to call them decent?"

"Well, they stand by the Yalta agreement and don't interfere with our internal affairs."

"And what about our belongings that they take over? What about our women, what about our mothers, our sisters, our wives, who are being raped every night? You call this Asiatic mob decent?"

Jozsi got up. I thought for a minute that he was going to slap Janos's face. He stopped in front of him.

"And I suppose that our decent, well-mannered, honest Hungarian troops, brought up on the teachings of Christianity, were celibate when they sneaked into Russia behind the Germans, eh? They always remembered the Ten Commandments when entering Russian houses: 'Do not steal, do not covet, do not commit adultery.' Oh yes," his eyes were bulging now and his nostrils quivering with rage, "our chivalrous soldiers defended Christianity and acted in the spirit of Jesus Christ our savior. Amen. I have photographs in my possession – pornography would be an understatement – photographs of Russians hanging from trees, and your Christian soldiers drinking to their death, no doubt saying Grace first. I have photographs of naked Russian women with bayonets protruding from their bellies, and laughing Hungarians standing by cracking jokes. I have addresses of people who brought home carpets, jewelry and God knows what else from the Russian front. I have a letter here in my case," and excitedly he pulled it out, "a letter from a Wehrmacht officer to his wife in which he says: 'God could not have created these Hungarian monsters.'"

An old man who had so far not taken part in the conversation, but had been sitting quietly writing in the corner, interrupted us:

"Come, come," he said gently, "what will happen to us if we fight amongst ourselves?" He went over to the window and looked out into the graying dawn. Then he spoke as if to himself:

"The trouble is that we always see the evil out *there*." He pointed towards the dark silhouette of the houses. "But the real danger is here," and he turned round and pointed towards his heart. "We have not grown up, that's the problem. We can only think in terms of murder, violence and rape."

We were silent, for we all respected the old man whose poetry we had read when we were in school. In the past he used to teach Hungarian literature at the local grammar school, but now he had retired to his books, his poetry and his still life paintings.

"The Russians," he went on, "have not brought anything in the form of horrors that is not already familiar to us. But perhaps they have brought with them something more important. I believe they have introduced the beginning of a new world, however distorted or confused it may be at present; and though the ideas may still be unconscious, they may prove to be the same ideas for which He died on the cross and which Christianity has chosen to ignore."

Then he went back to his desk and sat down again to write and dream.

It was already morning, and time for us to leave. I went to my office to write the leader. On our way Janos said:

"One of these days that old man will wake up to find himself in trouble."

"Typical condescending bourgeois talk. He is probably becoming senile," said Jozsi, spitting.

The title of my leader was *Britain's Answer*, and, naively perhaps (diplomacy and practical politics never being my strong points), I prophesied a Golden Age with Europe governed by democratic Socialism. The working people of Britain and the Soviet Union would together fulfill the dream of centuries: life without fear, without war, without poverty. I visualized Hungary for the first time in history as the bridge between the East and the West, the starting point of a democracy which would last for centuries. I finished my Utopian dream with the following comment:

> The eyes of History will not be blinded by Socialism wrapped in national colors, nor the ears of History deafened by slogans that only those hear who are unable to listen to the voice of life.

I felt very pleased with myself as I handed over the typewritten pages to the printers. When I showed my masterpiece to

Gergely he remarked quietly: "It's a pity you don't write poetry anymore." Jozsi said: "You completely lack all sense of reality." Janos made no comment at all.

The poet was still sitting in the room where we had left him earlier in the morning. I showed him the article. He read it through twice very carefully and then said:

"Like myself you are a poet, Jancsi. You should remain one. You dabble with things you don't understand. Dreams are seldom understood by those who do not dream."

I was bitterly disappointed by his reaction, and thought sourly that Jozsi had probably been right when he called the old man senile. I had no idea then that his few sentences were to become so significant for me later, and that circumstances were to prove him far from senile.

The next day I sat in my office as usual, opening the letters from our readers, and hoping that they would prove me and my sentiments right, when I came upon one which was unsigned and full of abuse. I concluded:

"You bloody bastard of a Jew, why do you preach your filthy democracy to us? Why don't you go back to your own bloody Palestine where you can preach to your own gang? You think your day has come. Well, we shall prove to you and to your rotten comrades that you are mistaken. Take care, Jew-boy. You will swing one of these days."

My secretary noticed that I had turned pale. I handed the letter over to her. She read it and her face flushed. "Mr. Heimler, there are times when I am ashamed of being a Hungarian. You should hand this straight over to the police."

I decided to do just that.

Later in the afternoon a detective sergeant called to see me. I started to speak: "I am sorry to trouble you with this business, sergeant, but…"

He interrupted me: "Mr. Heimler, I have no idea what you are talking about … I have a warrant for your arrest."

I thought I must have misheard him. He went on:

"This morning we received instructions from the Attorney General to arrest and question you in connection with an article published by your newspaper yesterday. I will read you the charge now."

I was charged with treason. The concluding words of my article: "The eyes of History will not be blinded by Socialism *wrapped in national colors...*" constituted "an attitude of vulgar defiance against the 1,000-year-old national colors of Hungary, written with intention to undermine the Constitution..."

"Mr. Heimler, I must ask you to accompany me to the police station."

I phoned through to Gergely and the others. Within a few minutes, with the exception of Janos, they all came. Jozsi said to the detective:

"You know what you are doing, sergeant? Do you realize that this is a national scandal?"

He said that he was only doing his duty, and that I must go with him. As I left the room my colleagues were already telephoning; no doubt with the intention of arranging my immediate release.

On the short walk to the police station, I asked the sergeant who the Attorney General was, and on hearing his name I remembered him: it was the same Simon Mihaly who, at the Gestapo's request, had signed the warrant for my father's arrest in the spring of 1944.

At the police station I signed a statement declaring that I had in fact written the article in question, but adding that nothing was farther from my mind than to defy the national colors of my country. The inspector in charge of my case was polite, but noncommittal. I was not locked up, but had to stay in his room. About an hour later he came in and informed me that on the telephoned instructions of the Home Secretary I was to be released immediately.

* * *

Jozsi was right. The affair developed into a national scandal. Apart from my own paper, some of the national dailies took the matter up and demanded the immediate resignation of the Attorney General. I had become a "local figure," and after the resignation of Simon Mihaly my articles started to carry some weight. Although the charge of treason left me with a very bitter taste, I refused to believe that a nation used to foreign masters would again choose Fascism now that she had freedom of choice, and I had faith that, with good leadership, perseverance and hard work, the nation could outgrow the memories and traditions of Feudalism, National Socialism and their attendant evils. I was willing to disregard my own personal bitterness and overlook the past for the sake of the future, in the hope that those opposing democracy would do the same.

I wrote articles in defense of those Hungarians forced by the Czechs to leave their homes in the reoccupied part of Slovakia: I exposed some officers of the new Hungarian Army who were stealing and selling food from the local military hospital where injured veterans of the Second World War were receiving treatment. I received a few letters from readers thanking me for my "patriotic" attitude, but the majority of letters were anonymous, vulgar and threatening. Some even went so far as to say that if I did not keep quiet I would soon be dead.

The Political Police, an organization recently set up to track down former Nazis, were powerless to find the writers of these letters. The attitude of the State Police was polite but uninterested. They could not, or did not, choose to do anything to help.

MY LIFE AFTER AUSCHWITZ

One evening I was walking back towards the flat I had now rented in Szel Kalman Street when two shots missed me by a few inches. The police said later that it was probably some drunken Russian soldiers "just playing about." I was convinced that whoever had wanted to kill me was not drunk, and that Russian soldiers had other things to do than hide in wait for me.

Shortly afterwards Jozsi came to see me at my home, and brought me a gun for a present, saying that it was time for me to wake up to the realities of life. He declared that the country was contaminated by Fascists, and that they were only waiting for the opportunity to strike again; that my dreams of democracy were the dreams of an idiot. Hungary was not ready for democracy. She needed a firm hand, and in his opinion the Communists were the only people whose hand was firm enough. If I did not realize this, then I was either a fool or else I had been so steeped in an atmosphere of bourgeois security that I was blind to it. He quoted a saying by Marx that the bourgeoisie could have no real identity with the working classes, adding, "but the bourgeoisie can have a good try."

As I listened to Jozsi I thought of the many that were, in his words, "having a good try." They came from varied backgrounds and had previously held many differing beliefs. Some were Jews who had returned from the death camps without relatives, wives or children and without a penny to their name, who saw Communism not only as a classless society, but also as a society in which race did not matter, who looked upon the Red Army as a new Messiah that would at last bring justice to this blood-stained earth. Others saw personal opportunities in this New Age, good jobs, responsibility and power, things that they had never had before. The Nazi sympathizers and the so-called "small Nazis" sought a hiding place where no further questions would be asked, and were they would be free from any possible retribution for their actions during the war years. Some joined in because they were genuinely disgusted with National Socialism and the destruction it had brought to the country.

But there were other members of the bourgeoisie who, in the sense of Jozsi's phrase, did not "try" at all. These were the spiritual descendants of the Christian Hungarian Monarchy, middle-class gentry, not necessarily Nazis, but faithful followers of the Admiral without a sea and his chauvinistic ideas. They had been brought up on the Numerus Clausus and other laws which penalized the Jews in various ways. These were people to whom Christianity had become a mere household word with little inner meaning. A great many of them joined the Smallholder Party. The Party leaders themselves were honest people, but the masses urged them to carry on where Horthy had left off. Their election posters bore the emblem of the cross, a sign which in different guises had appeared so often during political campaigns in previous years. Their meetings took place on Sunday mornings, after mass in the Square of the Madonna, and when the church bells chimed the hour of noon, the speakers made the sign of the cross over the assembled crowd and knelt for a moment before standing up to continue their attacks on the Socialists and Communists.

The Social-Democrats, on the other hand, were the proud bearers of a great tradition, who had been in existence for seventy-five years, and whose contribution to the nation included martyrs, philosophers and writers. Their fight had seemed a hopeless one, before and during the war against the Nazis, later against Capitalism and Feudalism; but their voice was the voice of freedom in the long night of oppression that darkened Europe. Now the Party had become "respectable," containing not only the many thousands who had remained loyal to its cause during the war, but innumerable newcomers, many of them opportunists who looked on the Social-

Democratic Party as a safe bet. The ranks of the Party, in fact, were split between those who wanted to carry out an independent policy of Socialist democracy, and those who felt that the country needed primarily to be built up economically and that only a United Workers' Party would be strong enough both to achieve this aim and to oppose the still existent dangers of National Socialism.

"You have written a political article," Jozsi said to me. "Possibly your intentions were good. Possibly. But who appreciated it? In fact, all you really did was to express your own individual problem, not that of the vast majority. You did not even voice the feelings of the Zionists, who most certainly have no delusions that when the new Labour Government comes into power there will be unrestricted emigration to Palestine and peace between the Jews and the Arabs. You stand alone. You belong nowhere. You may be able to use your pen quite skillfully, but you cannot write. A writer has to express the need of his time, to be the voice of the people. You are just your own insignificant voice.

He left in anger, but threw the gun he had brought for me on to the bed from the door.

"You silly fool," he said, "you may need this. No one else will stand by you."

After Jozsi had left me with the gun I sat beside my desk for a while staring at the alien object. Then slowly memories began to form. Was I five or six when my father brought me that black toy gun? For days afterwards I was the menace of the house, shooting everybody who got in my way. The rooms were full of corpses, who at my command came alive to be killed again.

"Doesn't he make enough noise as it is," my mother complained to my father in despair, "without your buying him that wretched gun?"

"Hands up, Mummy, hands up. Bang ... bang ... you're dead."
"Haven't you had enough, Jancsi?"
"Hands up, Daddy. Bang ... bang ..."
Guns were thrown away and new ones took their place. Broken guns lay in my drawer to be pulled to pieces and examined with fascinated curiosity.
"How does the gun work, Daddy?"
"You pull the trigger."
"But how does it work *inside*?"
One night I heard my parents talking over dinner about a client of my father's, a rich landlord, who had accidentally shot himself while cleaning his gun. Afterwards, when I was lying in bed, I pondered: "Can a gun *really* hurt?"

I received my answer years later, when the Germans arrived, and their guns with them. I was nineteen years old when they marched through the country towards Yugoslavia.

It was spring, and Count Teleki, our Prime Minister, shot himself because just a few days before he had signed a Treaty of Eternal Friendship with the Yugoslav Government. He died, and his death screamed to Hungary and to the rest of Europe that the Germans had come without his consent. That was in 1941, and we thought then that the guns had come to stay. But Hungary was not yet their final target. They had first to conquer the Serbs.

Then our own Hungarian guns sneaked past the Germans and over the dead body of Count Teleki. The Regent gave the order: "Hungarians, defend your southern border." And the guns went down to recapture what the treaty of Versailles had stolen from us, and at a place called Ujvidek, Hungarian guns shot the weaponless Jews and Serbs into the river.

Something dreadful and horrifying was associated in my mind with guns. In my own experience they had never been used for freedom and liberty, but always and only for hate and destruction.

The longer I stared into the barrels of those guns the more I hated them. As a slave in Germany I had sworn I would never use one. Now Jozsi's gun was there looking at me, a little black gun like the one I used to play with as a child.

Hours passed, darkness fell, and slowly the terrible symbolism of this weapon became apparent. I might have to use this gun any day, perhaps this very night or tomorrow, to defend my life and my ideals – ideals in which no gun had any place. "It's ironic," I said aloud, "really ironic that I should have to use a gun to create a gun-less society."

I got up and switched the light on, removed the bullets from the gun and threw them into the dustbin. But what could I do with the gun?

First I threw it into a drawer, then took it out and put it in the pocket of my coat which was hanging on the hook by the door. I removed it again, climbed up on a chair and put it on top of the wardrobe. But wherever I hid it, it was no good; as soon as I had turned off the light and got into bed, the cursed thing spoke to me, whispering words I did not wish to hear, until I thought I was going crazy. I got out of bed, climbed on the chair again, and squeezed the trigger of the empty gun in a frenzy of hatred. It clicked. God, the thing desired its bullets as a man desires a woman! I fetched the bullets from the dustbin and reloaded the gun. Then I put it under my pillow. But it was no good; it wanted to be held, and tightly held. "Kill or be killed," it spoke to me again and again.

It was not until the sun had dyed red the veil of dawn on the early autumn sky that I understood my own demented fear. It was not the gun itself that horrified me but the alternative it offered. Neither the written nor the spoken word, not courage, conviction or perseverance had the power to wipe out National Socialism: only this gun could do it. I realized

MY LIFE AFTER AUSCHWITZ

then that I was unlucky enough to have been born into an Age of Violence, and that my words had fallen on deaf ears. But I also realized that I too was a son of this Age, no different to the others. Horrified and afraid, with tears rolling down my cheeks, I had to admit that I myself was capable of using this gun, whether in self-defense or otherwise. The gun was silent now, but in the jungle within me everything that during the past few months had been denied and repressed was screaming to be let out. I sat there trembling, in the company of my own destructive, vindictive emotions, and let the hate come, let the beasts of the jungle loose.

When the storm had passed, I felt human once more. I undressed and while waiting for my bath to run I picked up an old prayer book. It opened at these words:

> Wash me thoroughly from mine iniquity, and cleanse me from my sin. For I acknowledge my transgressions, and my sin is ever before me...

Later that day, I returned the gun to Jozsi. I found him in bed, not alone, but with a naked girl who unashamedly sat up and smiled at me. Jozsi introduced us: "This is Comrade Szabo. Comrade Szabo, this is Comrade Heimler, better known by his pen-name, 'Comrade Vat.'"

I was embarrassed. I apologized for intruding, adding: "I knocked on the door, and thought I heard you say 'come in.'"

"That's right," laughed Jozsi. "You heard it all right; none of your bourgeois nonsense now. What's wrong with a man and a woman in bed?"

Comrade Szabo, exposing her beautiful breasts, laughed at my embarrassment, and asked Jozsi whether I had ever seen a woman before.

Jozsi yawned. "You see, Bozsi, since he returned from the camp, he believes in God."

"No!" exclaimed the girl, in mock admiration.

"Now, God says," Jozsi went on, "that little boys must not play about with such things."

Bozsi gave a scream. Jozsi must have tickled her under the cover. "And our Comrade Vat wants to be a good little boy."

The whole thing was ridiculous, and I wanted to get out as soon as possible. Bozsi with her naked breasts sent the blood pounding to my head.

"I came to return your gun, Jozsi."

Both of them burst into uncontrollable laughter, while I stood there stupidly pointing the gun at their naked bodies.

"So you came to return my gun," said Jozsi with mock seriousness. "Oh yes, I remember, the Ten Commandments forbid you to kill. Do they also say 'Don't be killed'? How are you, Comrade Vat, going to stop them killing you? Will the good book defend you?"

I had stood enough. I put the gun on the table and left. Their laughter followed me into the street.

CHAPTER THREE

Soon after this Jozsi was replaced on the *Free County News* and was expelled from the Communist Party. The same Jozsi who told me, "You don't belong anywhere," himself now belonged only to himself. He couldn't understand it.

Before August the Communist Party line had been clearly defined on the Party's attitude towards Czechoslovakia. They had openly condemned the deportation of Hungarian citizens as I had done. Then quite suddenly the Party line changed, and the deportees were branded as Fascists (possibly a great number of them were). Jozsi's article condemning the deportations was already set up in print, and next day it appeared in the paper. His expulsion from the Communist Party was based on his "individualistic" action and was one of the greatest blows of his life. He said he could not understand how the Party could make such a mistake; after all, he was one of those few men who had bravely confessed to being a Communist in the dark days of the Horthy regime.

We were sitting in my flat, and Jozsi continued to shake his head.

"I don't understand *them*, I really don't. So I made a mistake? Everyone can make mistakes."

"Why mistake?" I asked. "Haven't you an opinion of your own?"

"You don't seem to understand. We Communists do not believe in the opinion of the individual. If we did we should be in the same mess as the Social Democrats, with no cohesion, no unity, no sense of direction. There must be a body of people who have an overall picture of what goes on. If not, then everything will end in anarchy."

"So you still think you were wrong and the Party was right?"

"They must be right," he said, continuing to shake his head, "but I still don't understand."

"How could you understand if only the Party has an overall picture of what goes on? Perhaps the Party is wrong?"

"No. The Party can't be wrong."

"Are you still a Communist?"

"Yes, I am."

"But the Party says that you are not a Communist, and if the Party is always right, how can you still be a Communist?"

This shook him. For some time he couldn't say a word. Then he shouted with anger:

"I have a Communist past; I have been broken by a bloody rotten system. I have become what I am because those bastard Fascists and Capitalists made me what I am. The Party cannot wipe out the memories of my past."

"Easy now," I said. "Are you telling me that you are after all an individual? This is sacrilege."

As if he hadn't heard me he went on shouting:

"My father was a God-fearing peasant. He worked on an old Count's estate, and on Sundays he went to church and knelt before the altar praying for forgiveness for the Count who forced him to work and let him starve. My family lived in conditions that were so degrading you would never believe it, and the old fool knelt before the cross, and prayed: 'Lord forgive him, he knows not what he does.' But that old bastard of a Count knew only too well what he was doing. He was nearly seventy, and impotent except with very young girls. Everybody knew in the village that he bought those youngsters for his disgusting pleasure. He spent more on women and drink in one day than my family earned in two years – and my old man still prayed to God: 'Lord forgive him.'"

MY LIFE AFTER AUSCHWITZ

I wondered what this was all about, as Jozsi paced up and down my room like a hungry animal in a cage.

"When I was sixteen I still believed in that nonsense about God and all the other bull**** and one day I asked the village priest why he did not speak out against the Count, why he allowed the people to be exploited. I shall never forget the expression on his bloody hypocritical face: 'There is rebellion in your heart, my son. Go to confession, and ask God for forgiveness.' That was the moment when Christ died as far as I was concerned. Ever since then I spit when I pass by a church."

I asked him why he told me this, what it had got to do with his expulsion from the Communist Party. His anger turned against me.

"I tell you what. You have infected mankind with the curse of Christianity. The fellow on the cross, wasn't He a Jew? Didn't He preach the Gospel of your prophets and rabbis? I'll tell you why there is anti-Semitism in the world. Because of Him, because of that chap on the cross. Mankind hated His teachings, but the Church saw to it that no one rebelled against the 'Son of God.' So instead they rebelled against the people He came from, the people who have infected humanity with the curse of faith. Now don't interrupt, I haven't finished. A bastard named Goldman rents a nearby estate. During the war he and his family were hiding at a neutral embassy in Budapest. You could buy even life if you had enough money. Now he has returned, and every Saturday morning he goes to the synagogue with his dolled-up wife and children. From sunset on Friday evening until the Sabbath is out no one works on his land, because it is written in your damned Talmud that none of your menservants or maidservants should work on the day of rest. But do you think that he pays his workers for *his* day of rest? Of course he doesn't. He pays them for five days only because it is not written in your Bible that you must pay your servant in lieu of your fancy Sabbath."

"So Jews and Gentiles alike were products of a decadent age," I said. "What has all this to do with your present predicament?"

"I'll tell you what," he shouted at the top of his voice. "The clerics, the Fascists and the Jews have filtered into the Party machine to corrupt it from within. That is what has happened."

This time I was speechless, while Jozsi rushed up and down the room like a madman.

"Who ruled the country before the war, and who rules the country now? Look at the leaders of the Party today; Rakosi, a Jew; Gero, a Jew; Vass, A Jew. Yes, today they rule the country dressed in red, and yesterday the Wertheimers, the Goldbergers, the Weiss Manfreds ruled the country dressed in white. You Jews are clever, and very, very cunning."

I had enough of this and I said to him:

"It looks as if the Fascists have really broken you, not only in the way you think. They have broken your spirit too. The words you speak are not those of a man who has fought Fascism all his life. They are the words of Hitler and his gang. What can one expect from those on the other side of the fence, if you feel and talk the way you do? Perhaps your Party was right after all to kick you out, even if it was for different reasons."

He marched out of the room, banging the door, and he never spoke to me again.

* * *

I told myself afterwards that this was only one man, and that the forces of darkness could not infiltrate into every strata of our new society. I still felt that anti-Semitism was a sickness of our times and could be cured by the mutual efforts of Jews and Gentiles. One afternoon I talked to Janos about this. He listened carefully, and after some hesitation he replied:

"You look upon anti-Semitism as a pathological phenomenon created by the Gentiles only. That is not true. I go to church every Sunday, and every Sunday I am reminded of the cruel death that the Jews inflicted on our Lord. Who started anti-Semitism then? Did *we* or did *they*? There is something in the Jewish race that is really frightening. Their loyalty to an outmoded God has been a constant spanner in the Christian works in every age. Is it not strange that there has never been a corner of this earth where Jews were really liked? And that wherever they appear they infect others with the bacteria of hate? Forgive me for speaking so openly, I am sure you will realize that the very frankness of my words indicates clearly that I do not think of you as representative of your race..."

I listened with a pounding heart to the confession of this "Christian" before replying:

"What an old story that is: 'You are different from other Jews.' How often has that been said by Gentile to Jew, I wonder? Always it is the other Jews who are blamed, never oneself. You speak of a Christian age, but I find no Christianity in your words. Jozsi and you may use different term, but your spirit is the same. You talk of blame, of responsibility, implying that for the sins of fathers, sons of every generation will have to pay the price. But how do you know what are the sins of the fathers? How do you know that it was the Jews who crucified Jesus? Nowhere in the Talmud will you find that crucifixion was a Jewish form of execution. I do not believe in the sins of the fathers, but I do believe that sin belongs to all mankind. You see in the Jew all the ugly things that you won't admit to seeing in the Christians. A Jew was crucified two thousand years ago, and millions of other Jews have ever since been tortured and killed by those who called themselves Christians. What sort of Christianity is that, when you wash your hands from sin, like Pontius Pilate?"

I saw a faint smile appear on his face at the mention of Pilate. I went on:

"I want to forget the past and everything that happened to me. I want to help this country to stand on her feet again. How can I do anything at all, if my intentions are misunderstood, if my right to belong here is in constant question?"

Janos answered with quiet deliberation:

"You can't assist this country in her growth, because what *you* consider growth would be this country's death. You want a Socialist Hungary, but Hungry does not want international Socialism. Hungary wants to develop into a Christian Monarchy again. You will see the results of our elections. This country wants to go back to 1938 and carry on from there. National Socialism was an unpleasant interlude. This new Socialism will be an interlude too if *we* are allowed to have any say in our future. If that happens you will have no place here at all."

"When you say 'no place' do you mean no place as a Socialist or as a Jew?"

"Both," he replied, and left me alone to consider the implications of his words.

*   *   *

Was this to be eternally my fate? Must I wander until the end of time from pillar to post, finding everywhere the sign, *No Entry*? Are we, the people of my faith, to be punished in each generation for daring to give the world the Commandments of Sinai and the Sermon on the Mount?

Day after day I watched long columns of fellow Jews marching south across the countryside to the ports of the Mediterranean and the Black Sea. They were marching home to the Holy Land, without passports, without visas, not daring to mention their final destination, because the British were waiting with machine guns in the ports of Palestine. Once more the sign, *No Entry!*

One day a young man lay on the roadside in front of the house where I was living in the grip of an epileptic attack. The marchers stopped, searching the faces of the watching crowd. Then their leader made for me, as though he had recognized in my eyes our common fate. He asked if they could bring the sick boy into the house. We carried him up the stairs and laid him on my bed. And when it was all over and he had regained consciousness, his first words to me were: "Aren't *you* coming with us?" The others stood by in silence, but they looked at me in a way that made me feel ashamed. It was as though they were saying to me: "You are one of us. What are you doing here, away from home?"

After they had gone I opened the Bible and read the prophecy of Ezekiel:

> Prophesy therefore concerning the land of Israel and say unto the mountains and to the hills, to the rivers, and to the valleys, Thus saith the Lord God ...
>
> But ye, O mountains of Israel, ye shall shoot forth your branches and yield your fruit to my people of Israel; for they are at hand to come.
>
> For behold, I am for you, and I will turn unto you, and ye shall be tilled and sown:
>
> And I will multiply men upon you, all the house of Israel, even all of it: and the cities shall be inhabited, and the wastes shall be builded:
>
> And I will multiply upon you man and beast; and they shall increase and bring fruit: and I

will settle you after your old estates, and will do better unto you than at your beginnings; and ye shall know that I am the Lord.

By autumn there were no more marching columns. And on November 4, the nation voted by secret ballot. The right wing Smallholders received 245 seats, the Communists 70, the Social Democrats 69, the Peasant Party 23, and the (Liberal) Democratic Party 2 seats in the first free Parliament. According to a pre-election agreement a coalition government would be formed.

Janos was right. The past had won. That was the nation's wish. But the future stood at the gates with the Hammer and Sickle in her hand, and between the two there was only one bridge left, the Social Democratic Party of Hungary. In one last attempt to find my right place in this land, I decided to leave Savaria and go to Budapest.

*   *   *

During this period in Savaria, I had made only one real friend. Long ago he had been my father's friend, and recently during my days of conflict and despair he had helped me to see myself and my place in the world in a clearer light.

Before leaving for Budapest, I went to say farewell to him, and found him sitting by the open window overlooking the river, reading Stefan Zweig's book *The World of Yesterday*. He was a tall, white-haired man with large blue eyes; at over seventy he still possessed a remarkably youthful intelligence.

It was a Sunday afternoon of brilliant autumn sunshine, and as we sat by the open window, we could see the people strolling along the embankment in a leisurely way, and children running and playing in a near-by park. My old friend said he was glad to see me again, but was sorry to hear that I was leaving. "I realize that you must go, but I have a feeling that you may never return." Strangely he expressed what I was feeling myself. Then he changed the subject: "I hate these Sunday afternoons, it's all make-believe. Life is not quiet and peaceful like Sunday afternoons; it's grey and noisy, like Monday mornings, full of sweat and pain. And beyond the sweat and pain, there is always loneliness.

"You see, Jancsi," he said, holding up his book, "Stefan Zweig was right. One age has come to an end, and another is slowly creeping in: an age without feeling, brutally aware only of its own materialistic needs. The color and warmth of Stefan Zweig, the great understanding of Thomas Mann, are being superseded by the Iljah Ehrenburgs, who are ashamed to display their creative side. So instead they become glorified reporters. To them a color can only be compared to that of a steel erection plant, and the sound of the human voice to a vast electrical machine. And yet I can understand why they have denied that God in whose name the masses were kept in misery. All this time we have been talking about love, equality and better working conditions – but what have we done except talk? For centuries we have watched our peasants and laborers working themselves to death; we have allowed one and a half million Hungarians to emigrate to America; we have watched the blazing chimneys of the crematoria as if they were fireworks on St Stephan's Day … and we have talked, talked all the time. And what do we do now? We hate…"

There were tears in his eyes as he looked at me.

"You, for example. You have come back from hell, you have swallowed your pride and grief, and what do you receive in return? Hate, and more hate. You are a man who could have helped this nation to rebuild, but what will you do? You will leave and will take your abilities to a strange land, where they will allow you to use them. It's no use protesting that you are not leaving Hungary; you are only going to Budapest. I know you will leave in the end, because you must. No one will deport you or threaten you with the gas chambers again. But the day will come when you, and many like you, will recognize that man cannot live by bread alone; and then you will either have to fight or leave. And fighting will not achieve anything. Another war may destroy the world. The only way to win is to have a stronger faith. Communism is a new faith, and you can only conquer faith with a stronger faith. It may even be that the peoples of the East will themselves win by returning one day to the eternal values of mankind, having thrown away the hypocrisies of past generations. But in the meantime it is the task of your own generation to discover that stronger faith, not in the feudal god, not in a god who prefers the rich, but in God whom no man has created in his own image."

I had never seen the old man in such a state. He spoke, it seemed to me, like one of the old prophets of Israel; and yet he was a Christian.

"As this is the last opportunity I shall have of talking to you, let me tell you what I feel. I am saying this not only for your sake, but for my own, because there are few men to whom one can talk freely nowadays. You have told me often about the faith in God that sustained you in the concentration camp, and how you have now lost that faith. I am old and feel at times that I have lived long enough; when I close my eyes at night, I never know whether I shall see tomorrow's dawn. For a long time I have wondered whether there is more than this painful life, if there is something beyond the grave. In the past I have argued about these things intellectually, from the viewpoint of the class I was born into, and according to the ideas of my parents; but recently I have come to understand that the only way to find this eternal secret is not by thought, and not through talk, but by lending a helping hand to those who are in need. The act of man to his fellow men is the act of God. I realize too that I have failed like the rest of my generation to practice Christianity. But I also know that the very desire in me to have a God is a proof of His existence. Can you understand this? If you were raised, like Tarzan, away from all human influence, with no words to teach you, would you not know sexual desire when your body was ready for it? Would not your desire indicate, although you did not know it, that somewhere Woman must exist? It is the same with God. My wish for God is my knowledge of Him."

As we said good-bye, the old man held my hand for a long time.

"I will get in touch with you when you have settled down," he promised. He never did, because he died a month later of heart failure. But the words that he spoke the last time I saw him have remained with me ever since.

*　*　*

There are moments in life that are permanently photographed on to the film of one's mind in every detail. Leaving one's home, knowing that perhaps it will be forever, is such a moment.

The sun was shining, and a gusty November wind was bringing with it a promise of snow as I stood before the house where I was born and said good-bye. I had a feeling that everyone in the town was dead, that all the houses were dead, and that I was dying too. I walked away down the street and stopped at the corner. I looked back once more; never to forget.

This was my third attempt to leave Savaria. I had tried to get away twice before. The first day the car broke down. Next day I attempted to go by train, but for "military reasons" no train was running that day. Now a truck was waiting for me in the Square of the Madonna. As I settled down on top of the truck, which was carrying rubber tires to Budapest, I remarked to one of my traveling companions that it looked as though I might be fated never to leave the place. He laughed, and replied that from reading my articles he would never have guessed me to be superstitious. Almost immediately there was a sudden jolt, the brakes screeched, then came a bump, and we all fell on top of each other. Our driver had run into a horse, which now lay dead in front of the truck: the peasant who owned it nearly went out of his mind. He wept, swore, prayed, while someone from a nearby house telephoned for the police. For reasons still unknown to me, it was the Political Police who arrived, two plaincloths men on a motorcycle. Then followed a fantastic conversation, which I heard from the roof of the truck without being seen.

The first detective wanted to know why the driver was driving a truck. The driver said the simple reason was that he was a truck driver. The detective wrote this down. The other policeman then asked the driver where he was taking the truck and why. He replied that he was taking old rubber tires to Budapest, where he hoped to sell them. Why rubber tires? Why not? Why to Budapest? Because. At this point the peasant demanded that the dead horse, which was lying in the road, should be put on its feet. He had never had such a good horse, he said, and no money could compensate for it. Detective I said:

"You keep out of this." The peasant replied: "It wasn't *your* bloody horse, it was *mine*." Detective II reminded the man that he was not talking to other peasants, but to the Secret Police of the Republic, to which the peasant replied that no Republic had yet been declared, we were still living officially in a bloody Monarchy, and now the Monarchy had lost a horse. Detective I asked the peasant if he was trying to be ironical about the Republic. Here the truck driver intervened, asking: "Have you gone completely out of your mind, or can't you take a joke?" The peasant said he wasn't in a joking mood, and that anyway he was not interested in politics. But what about his horse? The detectives were not giving an inch, however: *they* were not interested in the horse. Why had they been called, they wanted to know.

Now Detective II had a bright idea. "I see that there are some people in your truck. Who are they, and why do they want to go to Budapest?" The truck driver shrugged his shoulders and suggested that the detective should ask us. We were invited accordingly to climb down, and a ridiculous interrogation followed. I decided not to give my name until the last moment, in order not to spoil the fun.

By now a crowd of peasants had gathered around. One woman "explained" to the others that some Fascists who wanted to get to Budapest in a hurry had run over the horse. That was why the Political Police had been called. Eight people, two to each leg, started trying to move the horse, but they were stopped by Detective II, who said that it was illegal to remove "a dead person or animal, or both" until the facts of the case were known. The women by this time were so angry with the detectives that they phoned for reinforcements, while the peasant sat by his dead horse and wept, watched by Detective I. In the meantime, Detective II was questioning the passengers. When it came to my turn, my conceit was hurt that obviously my name meant nothing to him. His next question surprised me:

"Have you any foreign currency on you?" he asked.

I was in the middle of replying that I had none, when the State Police arrived and got busy with the horse. They measured the distance between the animal and the truck (as the horse lay right under the front wheels there was no distance), then the distance between where the peasant thought he had been and the truck. While this was going on Detective I lay down in the road to rest, and Detective II, who had now lost interest in me, talked to the driver again.

"Have you permission to take these tires to Budapest?"

"Permission from whom?"

The detective did not know. At this point, the police sergeant came over to Detective II, and asked if he had any objection to the horse being moved. The detective said he would prefer if the horse could stay where it was until he had finished the questioning. After about half an hour, however, the "Politicals" and the "State" agreed that there was now a good case for removing the horse, so at last, two peasants to each leg, it was taken away, and Detective II gave us permission to carry on with our journey; all of us, that is, except the driver, who was held for further questioning in the matter of the tires. As the driver took the truck with him, we three passengers were left in the road, hoping for a lift. Eventually, a car came by and picked us up; and I arrived in Budapest the same afternoon.

MY LIFE AFTER AUSCHWITZ

CHAPTER FOUR

In Rakoczi Avenue, between the National Theatre and the Great Eastern Railway Station, stood the Palace Hotel. In the hall, where in the "good old days" travelers in underwear and paint had stretched out over a cup of black coffee, and uniformed porters had stood by the swing doors, another kind of man now stood in uniform. The new porters of a new age were the receptionists of the Central Secretariat of the Social Democratic Party of Hungary. In the bedrooms above, the officials of the Socialist movement worked where stolid burghers had once snored, made love, and washed their teeth, while in the front rooms, overlooking the busy avenue, sat Cabinet Ministers, Members of Parliament, the leaders of the new Republic.

This Party, although supported by less than seventeen per cent of the nation's vote, was nevertheless one of the most important political groups, having always represented in Hungary those democratic ideals more firmly planted in the soil of many other Western nations. Because of this it was continually under attack from both the Right and the Left.

In the dark corridors, professors rubbed shoulders with steelworkers, lawyers and businessmen with bakers and builders; Marxist theologians argued the maxims of *Das Kapital* with shoemakers from Ujpest, and alert young men stood modestly in the corners modeling themselves on the great.

But among this gathering of idealists, poets and visionaries, there were also some who had been sent to spy, to confuse and to betray, and with invisible daggers to stab this old noble movement in the back. It is small consolation, if any, that when they had completed their underhand work and had managed to push the Party into her grave, these traitors were also arrested, tortured and interned side by side with those on whom they had spied.

This was the building and the setting that I entered in the early winter of 1945.

* * *

The big city was in ruins. The splendid bridges, blown into the river by the Germans before they withdrew, lay like dead bodies with paralyzed arms pointing to the sky, and in their place Buda and Pest were now connected by only one insignificant wooden footbridge, hurriedly built on the site of the beautiful Bridge of Margaret, and known locally as the "Little Mary." The streets were unlit at night and seemed dark even during the day, not only on account of the heavy winter clouds that hung over the town, but also because of the gloom that emanated from the ruined houses, in which every household mourned for a lost relative. One was constantly asked the question that stabbed to the heart: "Tell me, comrade, what did they die for?"

It is not so hard to bear the pain over lost loved ones, if these have died for ideals they believed in. But if a nation comes to realize that her dead were sacrificed for devilish aims condemned by the greater part of the world, then these national martyrs died for no purpose at all. A nation may lose a war, her sons may be exiled, her women may be raped or sold into slavery, yet if the defeated nation knows that justice is on her side she can bear it all.

The great tragedy of my land was that although her poets and writers had lifted their voices throughout the centuries, yet because of her constant violation by East and West, the voice the world heard was not the voice of Jacob, but the voice of Esau. It would be easy for the West to say: "A hopeless nation, always violent." But when one sees a nation with her heart full of murder, one has to ask, who made that nation murderous?

"My dear sir," an old man said on the Russian front, "my daughter died in an air attack, my wife committed suicide, and none of us were Nazis or Fascist sympathizers. Who is responsible for it all?"

The question of responsibility, a constant theme of postwar years, is not as easy to answer as it might seem. "Of course, the swastika was responsible." But who introduced the swastika? "The Germans of course." And who allowed Hitler to come to power? "The Germans of course." It is easy enough to point the finger, whether at a man or a nation. One can, for instance, blame Versailles for the misery in Europe between the wars. But can wars ever be the work of one or two men, or one or two nations? Are they not more probably due to the unjust distribution of wealth in the world? Do not most men become animals when starved and defeated? Have we not learnt in the death camps that civilized man can become an animal when civilization is lost?

Old people were dying quietly in their little rooms that winter in Hungary, because there was nothing to eat; the workers starved because their money was not worth a farthing by the time they received their pay packets. And yet on the black market one could buy the impossible: butter, white bread, marmalade, meat. Who bought on the black market?

A desperate nation answered: "The lords of our new democracy – and the Jews, of course."

During the day, I worked in the Press Department at the Palace Hotel, reading the provincial papers and preparing resumes of interesting topics for the members of the Executive Committee. When some provincial paper was in difficulties I was asked to try to sort out the problems. I also wrote a few articles, but nothing of much value or interest. Since I had arrived in Budapest my pen seemed to have dried up.

During the evenings I enrolled as a student at the Academy of Social Sciences, a Marxist University, where I was taught to look at the world with new eyes. I was told, "You can only see the world from where you are" – the implication being that I came from a bourgeois family, and that anything I said or thought was colored by this inescapable fact. In vain I protested that I had a socialist background and that my father had identified himself with the interests of oppressed groups and the working classes: it was only too obvious to them that my father must have been "a bit woolly-headed," because he also attended the synagogue. Those who taught this stuff in the Academy were also products of the middle classes, but naturally enough they did not consider themselves to be "wooly-headed."

In the beginning, Marx created the heaven and the earth. And the earth was void; and darkness was upon the face of the deep. And the spirit of Hegel moved upon the face of the waters. And Marx said, "Let there be light"; and there was light. And Marx looked at the class struggle and divided the oppressors from the oppressed. And the evening and the morning were the first day.

Then Hegel spoke: "There is Thesis and there is Anti-Thesis, and out of these Synthesis will be born. But at the moment of birth Synthesis becomes Thesis, and so it goes on forever." And that was the second day.

Now history could be interpreted in a new light. Men were products of social conditioning, rulers were products of their time; and it could never be accidental that the inevitable happened. People were moved by their class interests, the oppressed rebelling against the oppressors and according to Hegelian principles becoming the Thesis, the ruling groups who in their turn oppressed others. The masses, like a magnet, attracted those leaders who expressed the desires of their followers. There was no place for accident or the whims of individuals; what happened had to happen. The human spirit was missing from this history. Thoughts, ideas and gods were all products of economic need. Sophocles wrote *Oedipus Rex* to satisfy the demand of his class; Shakespeare wrote *Hamlet* for the same reason. The creative element in man, all personal or spiritual inspiration, was absent from these teachings. If I stood up and asked these Marxist professors, "But comrades, why Sophocles? Why Shakespeare? Why did they not pick on someone else?" Surely personal gifts were a combination of hormones and other biochemical facts and had nothing to do with the matter under discussion. As I later found with the Freudian school, argument was only valid as long as one argued from their side. As soon as one took any other standpoint the answer was: "You see, you cannot understand, your very words of contradiction confirm that you can only see the world from where *you* are. You are in no position to criticize, because your criticism is a symptom in itself."

I once asked: "If human history is nothing but repeated class struggle, would it not logically follow, that the new classless society will eventually also produce its oppressed?" "No," was the answer, "A classless society will have solved its economic problems; thus there will be no more revolt, no more Anti-Thesis, no more war." This, then, was the age of the Messiah.

I asked: "How can the Hegelian philosophy be valid at a given time and not valid at another time?" The answer came immediately: "And does not Hegel represent his own age that is also bound to come to an end?"

And yet there was some truth in what they taught, even if it was only part of the truth. I could agree that man is conditioned by the forces of society and that the oppressed want freedom and fresh air; but I could not accept the view that past and present leaders of the world do not influence mankind, but are only influenced by mankind. Nor could I ever accept their view of man's role in the world as a little cog in the big machine, or agree that his only needs were purely materialistic ones. That Moses and Jeremiah, Jesus and Buddha, were products of their times I could believe; yet they made a mark not only on their own generation but on the many to follow by the very fact of being the personalities they were. These $a + b = c$ theories always left me uneasy and suspicious. Even if the church and the synagogue had become weapons in the hands of the powerful and spoke in the name of God to deny and misunderstand their spiritual creators, this could not invalidate on the grounds of logic the possibility of the existence of God.

* * *

I shared two rooms of a flat on the Great Boulevard with a boy from my home town whom I had accidentally met a few days after my arrival in Budapest. Steven was about my age and had spent the war years in a Hungarian labor battalion on the Eastern Front. During the last month of the war he had been taken prisoner by the Russians; now he worked as a tailor.

Steven, with a Jewish father and a Gentile mother, did not belong anywhere. He could not identify himself with the Jews because he was not brought up as a Jew; he could not identify himself with Christians because of what they had done to the Jews. He wanted to be a Socialist, but he could not accept Marxist principles. He was a lone wolf, tall and thin, full of conflicts, full of doubts, unable to take, unable to give. He had been a very different boy at home before the war; but the intervening years had broken his spirit.

MY LIFE AFTER AUSCHWITZ

But he needed me and I needed him. There were not many people left from our mutual past, and we both clung to a familiar face as if familiarity was the last hope.

Night after night I listened to his violent coughing. Each night he was sick, but every time I asked him what the trouble was he would become evasive and send me back to bed. One morning I did not hear him moving about and knocked on his door. There was no answer. I opened the door and saw him lying on his bed in a pool of blood. An ambulance took him to hospital, where for two weeks he lay unconscious before he died. The doctor said that he had cancer and must have carried for many months a terrible burden of pain.

It was Steven's death that opened up the blocked channel of fear within me. As though a tornado had descended from the blue, within hours my whole world lay in ruins. Nightmares flooded the dark of my nights, and in the mornings I awoke bathed in sweat. The depression that followed, the cumulative reaction to all that I had been through in the past, slowed me down to an extent quite unknown before, and with it came an extraordinary feeling of unreality.

It looked as if insanity was opening her arms to invite me to a final embrace.

* * *

One afternoon in the spring of 1946, when the world had become my world again, and the hills were green and the trees bowed their heads in the breeze, I sat with Lily in the grass on top of Mount Gallert watching the great river below that was like a ribbon on the city's dress. With trembling hands I gave her the first poem that I had written since the war, and when she had read the lines that she had herself inspired, I looked at her and spoke the words with which the world was created at the beginning of time: "I love you."

Lily was my second cousin on my mother's side. She was nineteen, with large brown eyes in which she carried a fire that was enough to warm us both. After my arrival in Budapest I had been welcomed by her family as a long lost brother.

She was to have been a pianist, but when the war came she had to leave the Academy. She had lost her brother during the war, and at first, I think, she looked on me as a substitute for him. Then, when my breakdown came, it was Lily who stood by me and helped me out of my darkness. Without her I would have been nothing. With her I could become everything.

When I was better I drove up to the Hill of Freedom, to a sanatorium where I could rest and plan my future. Friends in the Palace Hotel had made all the arrangements, and I was received with a courtesy reserved for the privileged.

The doctor examined me from head to toe before announcing his verdict:

"You are suffering from a reactive depression. It is not surprising that you should break down, after what you have gone through in the past years. Not to be normal at times, in an abnormal world, does not mean that you are abnormal, you know. You must rest, and walk, and read, and play tennis and swim, and you will find that you will recover very quickly."

MY LIFE AFTER AUSCHWITZ

CHAPTER FIVE

I had received a few dollars from my relations abroad, and with this hard currency in my possession, during the inflationary period, I felt immensely rich. I could now afford little luxuries like concerts, and occasionally a tea dance at the Majestic Hotel. The Majestic had been during the war the headquarters of the Gestapo, and the cellars still bore nightmarish memories of unspeakable tortures. Now jazz music had cleared the atmosphere, and even a few foreign visitors had appeared. During the afternoons the Majestic Hotel became my headquarters, as I hated to stay within the walls of the sanatorium, and in this bourgeois setting I used to dance with Lily and discuss with my Socialist friends the world to come.

I also made some new friends there, with whom I had an occasional drink. These foreign friends made a deep impression on my mind, for they were the first men I had spoken to who represented the outside world.

Rajah was an Indian businessman from Bombay, who was in the country to recruit Hungarian scientists for his firm that had something to do with electrical machines. Speaking in German, he would greet me every afternoon with the same words: "Hello there, my Hungarian friend! What do you think about the latest news?"

He knew quite well that I knew nothing about the latest news, because I had told him that in the last few weeks I did not read the papers or listen to the radio. But he waited patiently each time until I had said so before giving me his own news. "The British are holding up ships on the shores of Palestine again. One of the ships was kept at sea and the passengers and the crew started a hunger strike. Cyprus is one big concentration camp, and it looks as if the British will finish what the Germans started. They may think they are being clever, but they will find they are not: you can't piss against the wind, and the British in the end are going to wet themselves. India will be free very soon," he went on, "and then a new sun will rise in the sky of Asia. The British have been trying to stifle the breath of freedom in the world, but their time is up. They have done to India what the Germans did to Hungary."

"How can you say such a thing?" I said. "What did the Germans do but destroy? The British have built, organized and educated the country and changed the face of Asia. Where would India be without the work of those Colonialists? How can anyone compare the British with the Germans?"

He had a habit of listening very attentively, inclining his ear towards my mouth as if he was deaf, and would only answer after very careful contemplation.

"I was privileged," he said. "I belonged to a rich and educated class. I am half European, anyway, as my mother was a German Jewess whose parents settled in India. I appreciate the good things that Europe can offer. But what about the millions who have had no such luck? Are they more literate? Are they less hungry? Oh, yes, the British built beautiful houses, factories, streets – for themselves. Better ones, probably, than they had at home. But they have used India's wealth, labor and brains – for themselves. What about their treatment of Gandhi and other Indian saints? Perhaps one day" – a polite smile appeared on his face – "we shall be privileged to have you visit India. Then you will see things for yourself. You will be reminded of Auschwitz, I feel certain. There is no barbed wire, but while the British are there, India is no better than a concentration camp with its *Kapos* and other privileged prisoners. On the whole, the individual Englishman is a decent chap, with a sense of fair play, but in the mass, just like the Germans, they are bastards. The old rotten Colonial system has been responsible. Gestapo officers in British uniforms. *Herrenvolk*."

I said I could not believe that the British, with their traditions of freedom and democracy, could be compared with the Gestapo.

Again he listened carefully before going on.

"I knew a man, an Indian patriot, in the 1930s. He was jailed by the British but managed to escape. They recaptured him, and after that once a week they dropped him into an ice cellar where for twenty-four hours he lived on ice until his legs and arms rotted away. That shows you. India is not anti-white, and not really anti-British, but anti-Colonialism. One day perhaps the old wounds will heal, but a great deal will depend on whether the British depart gracefully. Within their island, of course, the British are civilized, but…"

I failed to hear his concluding words. I was thinking of the old man on the corner of the boulevards who had asked me not so long ago who was responsible for it all. The great jigsaw puzzle was now reaching its completion: it seemed as though the whole world was responsible – Germans, Hungarians, Englishmen, Americans, Russians. And yet something still puzzled me. How far does the individual influence events? How far is he able to say in the face of Nazis, Communists, Colonialists: "I go so far, but no farther. No matter what is done, I shall not kill, I shall not torture, I shall not inflict pain, even if I am considered a traitor for it."

Robert was an Englishman, a tall thin man in his late fifties, aloof on the surface, but when you got to know him you discovered he had feelings and intelligence. He never told me what he was doing in Budapest and I never asked. As Rajah would not talk to Robert, and Robert would not talk to Rajah, I had to transmit the conversation of each to the other.

"Of course there were atrocities," said Robert. "Man is the same the world over. But ... the Germans sanctioned brutality, the British didn't. The Germans were brutal on orders from above, but no such order came from any British Government. Bevin? Yes, his policy is an ugly one, but are things ever the fault of one man? I believe if there is anyone to be blamed, it is history itself. If you go to the Congo, the Belgians have a worse record than the British ever had, and the French too. Mankind has to go through a painful process while growing up, and Westminster can still offer something to the world. Without revolutions, revolutionary ideas have slowly shaped successive British Governments. We may have a long way to go still, but you should see it for yourself."

"Tell me, Robert, if I went to Britain, how would I be received?" Robert considered my question carefully.

"I have several foreign friends in England, who have all made something of their lives. It is not easy at first; language and custom can be tremendous barriers. But after these are mastered, it's up to you. Foreigners are not liked or disliked merely because they are foreigners."

I have never seen anyone drink as much as Robert. During our conversation he had managed to put down three lagers, and now he asked for a fourth. When he drank he could become quite intimate.

"'But don't go alone, John." (He had christened me "John," as he found Jancsi difficult to pronounce.) "You might feel very lonely if you went alone. Nowhere in the world can one feel as lonely as in England if one doesn't have friends. The fog, the rain, the long winter nights, the milling crowds in Leicester Square, all create a dimension of loneliness that might be frightening. It's frightening sometimes to the English, too."

*   *   *

MY LIFE AFTER AUSCHWITZ

During the long nights sleep often eluded me. What should I do? Where should I go? Should I go to Paris, the favorite of so many of our own poets and writers, or should I go to Palestine, to the original birthplace of my people? If I did that, would I have enough strength to fight again, perhaps with a gun in my hand? Or should I ask Rajah if I could go to India and be useful in some small way in rebuilding that tremendous continent? But each time my fantasy carried me across the Hungarian border, I found that I could not for long contemplate leaving altogether this blood-soaked Continent of Europe. Sometimes I wondered quietly whether I ought to go at all, but each time it was as though a voice answered from the distant past and encouraged me to leave: "Tear up your roots, Jancsi, get away. This is not your land; this is not your fight. They don't even want you here."

At last I applied for a British visa, for in the last analysis, it had to be England. Although what was going on in Palestine affected me profoundly, I wanted to go to England because it seemed to me that democracy was the nearest thing to a human Utopia. To obtain a British visa in those days was an almost impossible task, unless it was for the purpose of studying at a university. The British Council, which tried to help me, was in touch with some relatives who were already in Coventry, but they reported that unfortunately my relatives were in no position to assist me financially. This was the stumbling-block: how could all this be managed financially? Nevertheless, I applied for a three-month study visa, hoping that during that time I might be able to arrange something in England and learn a profession or a trade. When the visa was duly granted a strange mood came over me. Now that it was settled, I did not want to leave.

*   *   *

Apart from my belief in democracy, my childhood years also influenced my choice of England. My sister Susan, who was eight years older than me, had been a teacher of English, and had spoken it with no trace of an accent. She had an unusual flair for languages and spoke and wrote Italian, German, French and Hebrew, besides Hungarian and English. Towards the end of the war she started to learn Spanish, which she never perfected; in the gas chambers no books were allowed.

I was in my early teens when she began to teach English and French, and at my parents' request she started to teach me English also. I got no farther than the first two pages of the English primer, however; then I poured a bottle of ink over her skirt, slowly and deliberately, because I knew that never after that would she venture to teach me again. I also realized that I would have to atone for my awful act with a good hiding, which my father duly delivered. My mother scolded me, saying, "One day you will be sorry for your stupidity..." to which I replied politely, "Yes, mother," and went off to play football. And that was the end of my English lessons.

Now my mother's words came back to me, and I wished that I had never upset that ink bottle. I remembered the first few lines of Susan's English book, but that was all the English I knew. Looking back, I realize it was a stupid book, so unimaginative and boring that it would have needed the patience of a saint not to have become desperate. The book stated thus:

Teacher: "Good morning, boys. Good morning, girls. You are my English pupils and I am your English teacher."

Pupils: "Good morning, teacher. We are your pupils, teacher. You are our teacher."

*   *   *

It was not the English language then that had laid the foundation of my interest in England, but British history. In fact, though I had behaved so badly where learning the language was concerned, I could resort to blackmail to get my ration of history. I would say to Susan: "Does Mummy know that you were kissing a boy last night on the stairs?" Susan would blush and tell me to be quiet. Then, in the most natural voice in the world, I would ask her to tell me about the Magna Carta, or Cromwell, or Robin Hood or Oliver Twist (to me Oliver Twist was British history as well). She really was an angel; she always obliged. These stories made a deep impression on me and my father usually enlarged on them. In fact, I was surprised to find that he knew more about London than any other Hungarian I had known. He had an old picture book, containing many illustrations of London, and also a map of the underground system from its early days. On long winter evenings, he would sit with me for a little while and talk to me about "the greatest city in the world."

"You see, Jancsi, this is Hyde Park Corner." Then, pointing to another picture in the book, he would continue: "and this is a place called Marble Arch, where anyone can stand up on a soapbox and say whatever he likes."

"And what if he hasn't got a soapbox?"

"Then he can stand on a chair."

"Why does he stand on a soapbox, Daddy?" Father always got irritated by what he considered these irrelevant remarks of his eight-year-old son.

"What does it matter, in heaven's name, what the man is standing on!" Then I would keep quiet and he would calm down.

"The main thing is," he would go on after a while, "that there a man is free to say whatever he likes."

"Swear words, too?"

"Oh, don't be childish."

"But you said, Daddy, that he could say anything he likes?"

"Yes."

"Could he say 'silly teacher'?"

"He wouldn't want to say such a stupid thing."

"Could I say 'silly Susan'?"

But he had had enough, and that was the end of my English education for that evening.

* * *

I asked Robert about Hyde Park Corner. He was not much interested in the subject, but as usual he was obliging. His lack of interest, however, made me feel jealous for the first time. Here was a man who possessed a valuable diamond in his own country which he completely failed to appreciate. In that moment I understood what freedom really meant. It meant that one could get bored with it because it was a natural part of every day.

"Actually a lot of cranks speak there every night," Robert informed me. "Occasionally someone sane gets up, but most of them are cranks. Night after night they say the same boring things; they will even talk to themselves if no one else is willing to listen to them. Some even attack the monarchy."

So Robert thought the monarchy such a normal phenomenon that anyone who spoke against it must be mad. What a country!

On this subject Rajah also had his say.

"True enough, an Indian may say things in London that he would not dare to say in Bombay. England has built a system for the island's consumption only. It's not for export!"

I read Priestley, Cronin, H. G. Wells, even Jules Verne. I got hold of everything that was translated into Hungarian. It was Dickens who caught my imagination again.

"The implications are that only the privileged lived in freedom a hundred years ago. What about the rest?" I asked Robert.

MY LIFE AFTER AUSCHWITZ

"When the rest of Europe was treating men like slaves," he replied, "rows of houses were being built for the working classes in the reign of Victoria. In comparison, perhaps, we were somewhat more advanced than the rest of the world at that time."

"What about the children working in factories and mines?"

"I drove through your country the other day, and saw a great many children working in the fields. Nowadays in England children are no longer exploited, and they do not enter full employment until they leave school at the age of fifteen."

* * *

At night, during this period, I journeyed in imagination to England, and saw the small semidetached houses of the suburbs. I was always outside these houses, always alone, bitterly aware of my loneliness. This foretaste of my isolation, my inability to communicate my thoughts and feelings to my fellow men, made me feel despondent and frightened.

I started writing again. One after the other, my poems were accepted and published in the papers. It struck me then that giving up my Hungarian tongue might mean the end of me as a poet; that I might no longer want to write without my "reading public."

Often I have heard it said that the Jew has no loyalty to his native land, that he is only concerned with himself, his family, and his fellow Jews.

I was a Hungarian poet, proud of my Hungarian heritage and of the generations of ancestors who had lived and died in Hungary. I was proud of the Hungarian writers and poets of the past who had spoken of the eternal struggle of Man and of oppressed people: who had dreamed of freedom, of a life without fear. Perhaps it was because of my Jewish heritage, a heritage of pain, persecution and suffering, that I doubly identified myself with the tragedies of Hungarian history.

When I read the words of Hungarian exiles throughout past centuries, warning the country to resist invasion and to remain Hungarians at heart, I remembered the words of our sages who had warned Jewry since Babylonian times not to give in, not to lose faith, but to hope and believe in a better future. To me, being a Jew and a Hungarian was never incompatible.

But how much Hungary really meant to me only became clear during these summer months of 1946 when I knew for certain that I would be leaving her, perhaps never to return. During these weeks, I became aware of the language my mother had taught me, realizing that the language itself embraced her love and smiles, a thousand memories of precious years. To exchange this language for another one seemed like burying the beloved ones of childhood years. And with the funeral of one's native tongue comes the feeling of belonging nowhere. I felt the impending death of myself as a poet in the loss of these rich-flavored words.

At the beginning of September, I left the sanatorium feeling like a new man. The depression had lifted, the tiredness was gone, and the fear and restlessness had vanished also. My doctor gave me his final verdict:

"Your physical health is much better now, but the emotional wounds you have received in the past have left their scars. I cannot guarantee that the depression and anxiety will not recur. The only way to be sure of preventing a repetition of the breakdown you have experienced, would be to go under a prolonged psychoanalysis. Perhaps you may decide one day to do this."

My friends in the Palace Hotel had obtained a beautiful furnished flat for me on the Hill of Roses that once catered only for the rich. When I arrived, the garden was full of fading summer flowers and the view from the hill was unspeakably wonderful. Now that I was determined to leave, it seemed that I was being given every opportunity of settling down in comfort at last.

About that time, the United States had granted Hungary a loan of ten million dollars to stop inflation. A new, stable currency had been introduced, and once more we could plan to save money.

It was also possible now to plan with Lily our forthcoming marriage, and we arranged to be married on November 30. I had stood under the canopy of marriage once before when I had promised unending love to Eva, my first wife, who died in Auschwitz in the summer of 1944. Now I listened for the second time to the ancient words of the Rabbi, as if those words had come from another planet. There was something immortal in that painful melody: pain, beauty, strength, hope, all mixed into one. Like love.

* * *

Soon after our marriage I was compiling with Lily's help my third book of poems which was to be published soon, as by now my name was not unknown to many in Hungary. I had also just written a poem entitled "Gulliver" that received some publicity.

It was a symbolic poem that told the story of Gulliver arriving in the land of Lilliput, and of how, as soon as he was washed ashore, the tiny people put ropes around his neck because they were frightened of his huge size. Gulliver was Democracy, and Hungary the land of Lilliput.

The publication of this poem started a strange train of events that led me into a trap.

At a party I met a man I shall call "Uncle Zoltan." This was a nickname given to him subsequently by Lily and myself. During the evening he showed great interest in "Gulliver" and in my other poems, and told me that he would like to discuss with me the possibility of publishing my collected works. He even hinted that he might be able to produce a large edition, and of course I was very pleased with at possibility.

A week later "Uncle Zoltan" invited me for coffee at his flat. He was a man in his early fifties, of obviously high intelligence. We talked of poems at first, but soon the conversation turned to my parents, to my past, and to my beliefs. I had a strange feeling that I had met "Uncle" somewhere before, but however hard I tried I could not place him.

"So I gather," he said, "that you are not hostile to us?" He was referring to "us Communists," and obviously held a prominent position in the Party. He went on:

"You clearly recognize – and that is obvious to anyone reading 'Gulliver' – that Fascism is not dead yet and that it needs a United Workers" front to stop its growth."

I interrupted to say that nothing in "Gulliver" referred to a United Workers' front. He completely ignored my interruption, however, and continued:

"I am glad that you are not hostile to us. It would be surprising if you were, with your background and your father's aims. Your father must have been a man of vision."

Slowly he played on my emotions, on the feelings of a son for his father. The trap was set.

"Do you realize that reactionary elements have infiltrated into the very movement for which your father died? Don't you see that Social Democracy has become a tool in the hands of the Right wing? Surely it is your moral duty to expose these bastards?"

I said that I was not aware that my Party was being undermined by reactionaries. And even if it were, what did he mean by exposing them, I asked, and to whom?

"To us, of course. Because we have no Right Wing, and can trust our leaders who have stood the test of time in prison and in exile."

Suddenly I remembered why his features seemed familiar. In a flash it came to me that "Uncle," although he bore a different name, was the brother of the dictator of the Communist Party in Hungary.

At that moment I also realized that I had fallen into a trap. He was offering to publish my poems, and in return he wanted to use me as a spy against my Party.

My heart beat fast as I saw the danger that I was in. I had my visa for Britain, I had my passport, but I had not as yet obtained the necessary Russian exit permit to leave Hungary. If I refused him, it was not impossible that my Russian exit permit would not be granted. Did he know that I was going to England? It was only too clear that if he did not know yet he would know it soon enough. The system was such that spies were spied upon to test their reliability, and in his eyes, I was only a prospective candidate. From now on my movements would probably be checked. Although the State machinery was not yet entirely in Communist hands, the Political Police were certainly run by them. I had to make a decision quickly. Taking a bold step, instead of reacting to his suggestion, I replied:

"You may not know that I intend to go to England for a short visit. I have all my papers except my exit visa from the Soviet authorities. Could you help me to get this soon?"

He smiled, thinking that I was offering him a bargain. I was out of the trap, but this time he fell into it.

"You will get your exit visa within two days. Is your wife going with you?"

I told him that Lily would not be coming with me, and I saw on his face a sign of relief.

MY LIFE AFTER AUSCHWITZ

"You go to England, and when you come back we shall discuss further the publication of your book."

That night I decided to tell a veteran Socialist of the conversation that had taken place between "Uncle Zoltan" and myself. He was not surprised. He said:

"You are not the only one they have approached. But certainly you are one of the few who has reported it to me."

* * *

At last the day came when I had to say farewell to Budapest. I felt on that winter morning that I was like a man who is about to jump into a swimming pool, uncertain if there is water in the pool. I was about to leave behind everything that I had valued since my early years. The offer of fame, the opportunity of comfort, but above all, my young wife. My thoughts were uneasy and my heart beat heavy under my winter coat, as I sat in the taxi on my way to the station where my wife and friends were waiting to say goodbye. I had left my passport at the travel agency where I had collected my ticket an hour earlier, and I was racing back now from the agency to the station watching the cold streets and the sparkling snow. I looked at the Danube for the last time. Would I ever see it again? Goodbye, Budapest. Goodbye childhood. Goodbye girls. There was a crash, and my head receive a heavy blow as I fell backwards. We had collided with a van. Police. Names. Numbers. No serious damage, thank God, but time is getting short; the train is due to leave soon.

Into another taxi, shaken, frightened, heart palpitating.... The second taxi had not traveled a mile, however, when there came another crash on Rakoczi Avenue. This time two taxis had collided with each other and we had run into the rear of one of them. Police. Names, Numbers. No injury. Trembling, in a cold sweat, I ran towards the station, praying as I ran:

"Oh God, let me go, let me go at last."

MY LIFE AFTER AUSCHWITZ

Quick kisses, handshakes, a few tears – and the Alberg Express was moving slowly towards the West. Goodbye to Lily, looking like a doll in her white fur: "You'll join me soon. Good-bye, goodbye…"

PART II: GREEN GRASS and FOG

CHAPTER SIX

In a small dirty hotel room near the Gare du Nord, a grayish patch spread its tentacles in all directions just above my head, reminder of a burst pipe or perhaps an overfilled bidet in the room above. The wardrobe was an old-fashioned one: there was a key in the lock, but it had stopped functioning eons ago and a newspaper dated July 3, 1946, was fitted between the doors to keep them closed.

Beside the wardrobe was a wash-basin, with a cracked mirror, and a bidet. The large bed would comfortably have held both Lily and me, and I thought regretfully that I should have to be alone. God knows how many lovers must have shared this bed in bygone years. One naked electric bulb hung from the ceiling, cold and unlit in the early winter evening. Over the orange chimneys of the houses opposite I saw the top of the Gare du Nord, from which came the occasional whistle of a train. Then the light grew faint and the shadows fell, and when the early February night had covered everything in darkness, I was still lying on my bed unable to believe that I was in Paris at last.

Pali was a violinist who came from my home town and had lived in Paris since the end of the war. He took a special pride in showing Paris to me, the "foreigner," for he knew well how it would thrill a Hungarian poet's heart. We visited Notre Dame and discussed the beauty of a bygone age when Man's mind still soared towards heaven; we gazed at the unspeakable glory of the Saint Chapelle; and from the top of the Eiffel Tower we looked down on the great city basking in the winter sunshine.

He took me to Montmartre, and we watched the contortions of naked bodies in the tiny theatres there. But he showed me the other Paris, too, of those who live on the Left Bank of the Seine. There he lodged with another Hungarian, a photographer by the name of Feri, and a Frenchman in his late forties called Monsieur René. While my Hungarian friends called themselves artists, and no doubt were accepted as such by other members of the Quartier Latin, Monsieur René was an outsider because he worked for the Ministry. His greatest ambition in life was to look like an artist, however, so he grew a moustache and a beard and after office hours dressed in the rags of the intelligentsia, claiming that he was an artist without an art. He also claimed that he was a direct descendant of François Villon, "on the bastard's side, of course," and pointed to the pagan romanticism in his veins as the living proof of this. This flat in fact belonged to Monsieur René, but in the passage of time most of the furniture had disappeared. All three agreed that one did not require much to be happy on this earth; one only needed drink, and food, and women, and a bed of course – and fame. The only one who had made a name for himself was Feri. His photographs of naked women, he would say, were no ordinary studies in the nude but "symbolic expressions of the relationship between woman and the universe." He explained that every woman since the beginning of time had retained in her facial expression and movement something of an animal, and that his primary function as an artist was to catch and express that animal.

Sitting in the local bistro, he would watch every woman who passed by, commenting: "Tigress, cat, dog, swine, vulture, fox..." When he had selected a model, he would undress her, place her on a rug, and then get her to take up the pose, as he conceived it, of the appropriate animal.

"There is only one expressive pose for any given woman," Feri would say. "A dog-woman must adopt an entirely different pose to that which suits a tiger-woman. The success of my art lies in the recognition of these basic facts."

This short stay in Paris was my first taste of freedom, and I was grateful that the first stop beyond my country's borders should have been with this gay and friendly crowd. It gave me hope that across the Channel I might also find echoes of a familiar life. Paris, pleasurable though it was, was merely the bridge between the old life and the new. I walked for the last time down the Boulevard Saint Michel, where once the great Hungarian poet Ady had met the phantom of death one autumn afternoon. Then I hailed a taxi and drove to the Gare du Nord, en route for the land of fog and green grass.

MY LIFE AFTER AUSCHWITZ

CHAPTER SEVEN

On February 11, 1947, I arrived in London, I wrote to Lily. Behind this laconic announcement lies a whole new way of life.

Victoria Station in darkness.... An old porter saying "Ta" as he takes my luggage, and "Ta" again when I utter my first English words, "Taxi, please."... The taxi racing through the night, with the driver muttering under his breath.... Freezing cold outside, no green grass, but fog all right.... Traffic lights changing mysteriously (this is a new sight; in Budapest police control all the traffic lights)....

The first English words: ration card, power cut, how do you do? How are you? They don't make sense. The soup ... you move the spoon away from yourself; only the second movement is aimed at the mouth. Why don't they put the peas on the inner curve of the fork, instead of attempting the impossible by trying to place them on the outer curve? Why do they eat bread and butter with their soup? Why do they say "Uhmm. Well..." when they don't want to answer you? Why the ceremonial dance when you walk with a woman in the street and you must keep always next to the curb?

Are they incapable of saying what they think? "Perhaps I might suggest, Mr. Heimler..." What does it mean? Does it mean "You do it, or else...?"

The struggle to learn the language, trying to put words together into sentences and then "tuning" one's ears to understand what is behind the words. "He is not particularly brilliant." Does it mean that I am just a little less than a genius or do they consider me an idiot?

The little grey book says "Aliens Act 1921." I look up "alien" in the *Oxford Dictionary*: I want to know what I am. "Not one's own"; "foreign, under foreign allegiance"; "differing in nature"; "repugnant…," that's what I am. "Repugnant," "excluded," "hostile." And "alienisms," according to the same dictionary, means the study and the treatment of mental diseases. This can drive anyone mad.

The first impressions have worn off and now life is very lonely here.

Oh Lily, Lily, when will you come? Here in this strange country I feel so lonely amongst the crowd. Robert was right; this is the loneliest city in the world. Summer has now come, and people are out on the streets. I see couples in the park embracing and loving, and men sitting with their wives over a glass of beer. I am hungry for affection, for the touch of love. I cannot sleep at night. When will you come, Lily, my love?

I begin to meet people, foreigners like myself, but most of them I dislike. They tell me: "Like you we were also deported, to the Isle of Man." I have to smile. They spent the war years in hotels. Some of them are left-wingers and Communists, who now want to return to the paradise at home. When I tell them that the paradise has been lost, they call me a Fascist warmonger.

I am afraid of what might happen to you, Lily. I hear that the clouds are gathering in Hungary; that people are being arrested every day; that even our Prime Minister has resigned. When will you get your passport, my love?

I have applied for a temporary job with the BBC.

Aldwych. Bush House. Hungarian Section. This is London, here is the news: "It has been reported from Budapest that Bela Varga, President of the Hungarian Parliament, has left the country." I smoke a cigarette as the microphone stares into my face. Lily, do you hear my voice two thousand miles away?

MY LIFE AFTER AUSCHWITZ

"The Under Secretary of State wishes to inform you that a visa has been granted to your wife."

So, Lily, you are coming at last!

* * *

It is the end of 1947, New Year's Eve, and we are sitting in our dark room in Kingdon Road. Lily has just come back from work. She works in a bakery in the West End. She is tired, unhappy; so am I. I live on what she earns and she lives on tears. This is not the way she imagined it at home. We have no money to go anywhere, and anyway we don't know anyone, people don't know us.

I have been writing all day and now I sit and stare into nothingness. I am writing a book on my life in the concentration camps, but I find that when I have to step back into the past and live again those fateful days, trying to see the world as I saw it then, something holds me fast in the present, for the past is full of pain and I do not want to suffer again.

"What shall we do?" I ask.

"What can we do?" she says, sitting on the bed. What can we do? The borders have closed behind us now. We cannot return.'

"But this is no life for us, me here sitting in this room, waiting for you to come and then not being able to speak to each other because we are both too tired."

"If only you had succeeded with the BBC."

We had discussed many times my interview for a permanent job with the BBC, and how I had failed.

"My English wasn't good enough for them."

"You made a mess of the whole thing. It wasn't only because of your English that they turned you down."

She is right, of course. I had made a mess of that interview because I had been afraid. Now I tell her for the tenth time what happened.

"I thought that they were following me. For several days I had seen two men, sometimes driving in a car, sometimes walking behind me in the street. I thought that 'Uncle Zoltan' had sent them after me. I could have sworn that they were up to something. I told you that at the time."

"You were imagining things. You are not as important as all that, even if you like to think so. But here no one knows who you are, what you are. You made a mess of it."

I had made a mess of it all right. All the time I was before the interviewing committee I felt as if Uncle's spies were standing behind the door listening to every word I said. I did not dare to say what I really thought, or show any interest in politics; I made myself out to be a fool who was interested in poetry and nothing else.

"What can we do now?" I ask, and Lily sits on the bed and repeats mechanically: "I don't know, I don't know, I don't know."

As we sit there, the clock moves towards midnight. A New Year is about to begin. What fresh pain will it bring us? The chimes of Big Ben come over the radio ... nine, ten, eleven, twelve.... People are singing and dancing in Piccadilly Circus. We do not sing, we do not dance ... we go to bed facing our private darkness.

Where are the hills of Budapest? Do they still stand above the Danube? Does the field of faded grass in which I declared my love for Lily still retain an imprint of that day? Where is our love now? Have tears washed it away?

*   *   *

During that spring I was troubled by dreams. Now that the spies no longer threatened from without, "Uncle Zoltan" threatened from within, accusing me of being a traitor to my homeland, and to the memory of the millions who had died during the war. When I awoke in the middle of the night I felt guilty for having used him, an enemy, to bring me to England, and every aspect of myself that was at war within me spoke with his tongue; until at last I realized that he was merely a symbol of my own inner darkness. At that moment of crisis, to be a Jew was a great help to me. I recognized my own trial as but part of the trial of centuries, and by identifying myself with my persecuted people, my pain became a link in their chain.

It was at this time that the State of Israel was being reborn from the dust, and on long sleepless nights I thought of the prophecy of which I had first heard in Savaria. What were the forces behind history? Was the creation of Israel nothing but the result of fanatical belief, a kind of self-hypnosis, or was it more? Was I witnessing in the wilderness of modern life the fulfillment of God's promise as it was written thousands of years ago?

I felt in my blood and in my brain cells that I belonged to an indestructible people. And this belonging helped me to gain new hope to face the trials of my present life, to stand up, to fight again, and not to let myself be beaten.

* * *

During that year, with an unparalleled effort, I learnt English, wrote my book and attended lectures at an evening class of London University. Also, for a short time I earned a few pounds. The Hungarian Embassy needed part-time workers to register British claims for shares lost by nationalization. For a few weeks I felt I was on Hungarian soil again. But it was soil that trembled under my feet. On July 30, the first President of the Hungarian Republic, Zoltan Tildy, resigned and his son-in-law was arrested and sentenced to death on charges of high treason and espionage. When the guillotine finally fell on the last remnant of Hungarian Democracy, I was back again in our little dark room, and the only thing I could look forward to were Lily's homecomings and our weekends together.

*   *   *

One Sunday afternoon in July we went to Hampstead Heath. Sitting there in the grass we watched the "Sunday people," who are the same all over the world. There was something in their slow movements and in their tired gestures that reminded me of a film in slow motion. As the hours passed, I slowly became aware of the miracle of air and wind, of a purpose in life not always recognized by Man, and the words of the Psalmist came suddenly into my mind: "Oh Lord my God, in Thee do I put my trust: save me from all those who persecute me, and deliver me…"

I laid my head in my wife's lap, and felt the shadows of my dark nights gradually evaporating into the great blueness of the sky above. "I cried unto the Lord with my voice and He heard me out of His holy hill…"

When Lily and I got back to Kingdon Road that night, we found that we had lost our keys. They must have dropped out into the grass as we got up to leave for home. We could not get into our room without them, so we had to return to the heath. To find small keys with the night coming on in the grass of an immense field is an almost impossible task. Was it through this small opening here that we had entered the heath? And was it under that tree over there that two girls were eating their sandwiches a few hours ago?

"No," Lily said, "it wasn't here, but a bit farther up. Oh yes, a dog was doing his business under this tree. Now look for that." And there I was in the night on a large heath, looking for the excreta of a strange dog.

Lily found it first, and called to me with great excitement in her voice. She had found it; she had found the dog mess. We walked in circles for some time. No keys anywhere.

"How could we *both* lose our keys? It doesn't make sense. It was completely mad to come back; we shall never find them in this darkness."

She reminded me that we had already found something: the droppings of the dog.

I was rather concerned about the police. If they spotted us in the middle of Hampstead Heath in the dark, what conclusion would they come to? My imagination ran loose.

"Look, love, someone may have picked up the keys. You know what people are. These British particularly, they collect everything. The chap who picked it up may collect keys. Who knows? Please let us go home, and break the lock...."

"No. Anyway you are talking a lot of rot. No one would collect keys."

"From now on, I am a key-collector."

"Please be quiet."

"Oh, hell...."

Hardly had I uttered these words, when she turned to me.

"Are you swearing at me?"

"Of course not, love."

"You were. I am doing all the dirty work here, and he is swearing."

When Lily referred to me in the third person, though no one else was about, I started to laugh, and laughed until the tears rolled down my cheeks. I could not stop.

She was now on all fours, almost crying in her despair.

"They're not here. All right, you win: I give up."

But the laughter had washed away my bitterness. I was now quite prepared to spend the night here, and next day, and the whole of next week, to find those keys. I knelt down beside her in the wet grass, and said:

"Don't you see, this interlude here on the heath is life? We look for something that we have lost. We try to find our way in the dark, and what do we find? A dog mess. You go on your way determined, while I dream. We quarrel; I laugh; you get wet and your dress gets dirty. Now I am not going to let *you* give up; *I* am going to be the strong one. And now I shall kiss you, not only because this night is highly symbolical, but because I want to." We kissed, kneeling in the wet grass, forgetting about policemen, the dog mess, even the keys.

"I love you, you silly thing," I whispered into her ear. "I love you even if I never find those keys."

And then the miracle happened. As I moved nearer to her, I felt something hard under my knee. I knew it was the keys, but I finished kissing her first, before I picked them up and displayed them in the light of the moon.

"I love you," she cried happily. "I love you..."

As we went home, we both felt that somehow we had solved a problem. We had been looking for something, and we had found what we sought. Not only the keys to our room, but something more. We had proved that night that however impossible a task may appear, if there is will, love and laughter, even tears, it can be achieved.

*   *   *

After this, with strength renewed, I tried my hand at many things. For a time I was a traveler in books for a continental publisher; I was a reader for another; then I became a photographic printer, and then a postman. I could speak English now, and was ready to sow the seed blown here by the storm firmly in British soil. Before, however, I could dig up my old roots I had to face my inner world, which was sending uneasy messages to the surface. I was determined now to dig up the past and to get rid of it forever. And so, remembering the words of my doctor in the sanatorium on Freedom Hill many summers ago, I decided to undergo psychoanalysis.

MY LIFE AFTER AUSCHWITZ

CHAPTER EIGHT

My decision to seek help crystallized during the summer and autumn months of 1949. At this time news was arriving from Budapest of the arrest of my old friends and comrades, of tortures by the Secret Police, of the end of Hungary as an independent State. On August 20 a new Constitution was declared by the puppet parliament, very much on Soviet lines. A "night of long knives" fell on Hungary, and I could not dream any more about my eventual return. The realization that I was now completely cut off from my native land, together with my grief over the many brave men and women who were facing death, and the shocking realization that this would have been my fate too had I stayed behind, triggered off an immense despair.

On September 23, with my ears glued to Radio Budapest, I heard the voices of some of my friends, as the "Trial" was broadcast to the world. They all confessed to sins that would have been impossible for them, and sometimes referred to matters that I myself had known of, and about which I knew they were not speaking the truth. I did not have to stretch my imagination far to realize how these "confessions" came about. I saw in my mind's eyes the flesh-torn bodies, the unbelievable cruelty of a new Gestapo. The Holy Inquisition also tortured people in chambers of horrors with acts against humanity. But in those days there were some who, tortured and broken, still declared their innocence before the priestly judges, their belief in God and Man. What a difference between the trials of the Middle Ages, and those of our twentieth century. Now everyone confesses, everyone cries: "*Mea*

Culpa, mea maxima Culpa!" How far can man destroy man's mind and spirit? How far can Evil rule the world?

I telephoned to a well-known psychoanalyst to ask for help, telling him that I was now a refugee; that I had no money to pay for treatment, but that I needed help very badly.

He saw me next day, and once or twice more. He was warm and kind, and promised to arrange a full analysis for me with another psychoanalyst in the West End. His parting words remained with me: "You will learn, you will begin to understand, and if everything goes well you will grow." He also hinted that although my experiences in the concentration camps might have triggered off my present unhappiness, with the Rajk Trial as the final straw, yet he thought that the cause of my trouble went deeper than these.

*   *   *

My first encounter with psycho-analysis goes back to the years of puberty, when, to find the answers to the burning questions of those times, I read everything I could, regardless of whether I understood it or not. It was Stephan Zweig who introduced Sigmund Freud to me in his book, *The Healers of the Mind*. The life histories of Mary Baker Eddy, the Christian Scientist, Mesmer, the mystic hypnotist, and Freud aroused in me then an interest in the human mind which has never faded. Freud's life, his struggles against the narrow-mindedness of his age, awoke in me great sympathy for this man who had dared to pioneer deep into the jungle where no man had been before him. Poets, writers, and artists of all kinds had dreamed about this jungle since time immemorial, but Freud did more than dream; he went out to face the beasts and the mud, and by doing so he risked a great deal, including his own sanity. In a world in which man saw danger only in others, he dared to declare that man's chief danger lay within himself. Believing in no God, but only in what he could prove, he yet conveyed the same message as those prophets and saints who had commanded man: "Know thyself." Risking ridicule and the loss of financial security and professional status, he ventured into the land of dreams, where only cranks, mystics and prophets had been before him. On this "Royal Road," as he referred to dreams, he entered the jungle and tried to map its chaos. Stephan Zweig told the story of Freud as a man who ventured into an invisible land, and returned each night to his wife, to his children, to society. Because he talked of sex, and because sex had become the taboo of the Judeo-Christian civilization; because he dared to show that sex and love are intertwined, like the mysterious roots of jungle trees, he shocked his generation, who were unable to accept the idea of love in sex. Reading his books and those of his disciples, my adolescent mind, without understanding everything they contained, instinctively accepted his claims.

My generation of Hungarian Jewish middle-class adolescents, born after the First World War, looked mainly towards the West for their answers; and Freud's ideas were accepted by them without question, for the spirit of freedom emanated from his words. We also turned for the same reason towards the Paris of Baudelaire, Verlaine and François Villon, towards the Moulin Rouge and the Casino de Paris, because they were all daring in an undaring age. We were "angry young men" with a difference. We not only said: "This is rotten and bad; we also turned to that of which we could say: "This is good, this is what we want." We wanted the democracy of Westminster and Petrarch's sonnets and Nietzsche and Cicero, the *Divina Commedia*, Thomas Mann, our own poet Ady – and Freud. Freud might have seen in our wide intellectual interests a kind of neurotic escape, because we did not want to face the obvious dangers of our times. Yet, there was something more. Man short of air must use any available source of oxygen if he is to remain alive.

MY LIFE AFTER AUSCHWITZ

By the time I matriculated I considered myself a "Freudian," looking at the world through Freud's eyes. How far I succeeded I do not know, but I do know this: I had two ambitions during those years, to become both a writer and a psychologist.

*   *   *

My analysis started in January 1950, and I attended five times a week, for fifty minutes each time. My doctor was a woman in her sixties, of foreign origin, but she could not speak Hungarian. As I did not wish to relate my past and my feelings in German, we agreed to speak the language of our adoptive land, so English it had to be. This produced in the end a most interesting result. As I was relating my life in English and therefore translating my memories into another tongue, the emotional ties that bound me to Hungary, particularly to the Hungarian language, became in the end relatively unimportant, and my memories, although experienced originally on Hungarian soil, now became those of a man for whom that soil had lost its significance. By the strange metamorphosis of psychological chemistry, my thoughts and dreams have ever since been expressed in English in all the layers of my mind, and although my English is far from perfect even today, if I ever speak my native tongue I have to translate from the English and therefore make many grammatical mistakes. Although I have retained a Hungarian accent, after my analysis I was no longer aware that I spoke differently from my fellow Britons, and most of the time I am now unaware that I am still a foreigner. The effect on one's national identity of psychoanalysis conducted in a different language from one's own has to my knowledge not yet been investigated.

On my first visit the doctor told me to lie down on a couch, instructing me to say anything that came to my mind, however irrelevant or silly it might sound. She said that I should have to do most of the talking, and that only here and there would she comment on what I said. During our sessions she herself would sit just behind me.

To reproduce an analysis is impossible; all I can attempt is to give the "feel" of it. I will go as far as I can, and I shall be as honest as I can. But there are areas in everybody's life that are not for public viewing: I will only touch on these, and will leave it to the reader to draw his own conclusions.

* * *

"This room ... it's a small room. You shouldn't be working in a small room like this. You should be working in a big room, the kind one sees in American films. Nobody will think much of you if you work in a room of this size. I hope you don't mind me saying these things, but you told me to mention everything that comes into my mind. I wonder what you keep in your drawers. I bet you keep your drawers locked, so that if you go out to spend a penny you can make sure that I shan't look into them. You have your secrets, I have mine. We all have secrets.'

"What secrets?"

"Secrets, that's all. There are small secrets and big secrets. When you are small, the secrets are small, although you may think at the time that they are big. When you grow up you look back and laugh. You have real secrets now, and those secrets were unimportant. I know you have your secrets too. Some are locked in your drawers. What do you keep in your drawers? I asked you a question. Why don't you answer me? Now I don't feel like talking to you at all. Not at all. It's ridiculous, that I should ask you a question, and all you do is to sit, like an all-knowing goddess. I feel unhappy now, I don't know why. This room is small, everything in it is small. I feel small, too."

I am looking at moving pictures now, as though at a film. They pass quickly, but I see them very clearly indeed. She asked me to tell her everything but I cannot tell her about these pictures. By the time I could speak, they would be gone. How can I tell her everything: She must be mad. I told her that I felt small. Well, that is how it seems. Between the desk and the door in midair. It's a hotel room. Where? In Italy. Where in Italy? I don't know. There is a large bed in that hotel. I am alone in it. Mother and father went out and left me here all alone. They go out every night, and they always leave me alone. The window is open, and I mustn't put on the light, because strange creeping things might fly in through the window. They might fly in now. If *they* were here with me, nothing could get in. They are coming in, because *they* went out. They are always going out. It's a very big room, too big. The bed is too big, too. The sea makes funny noises out there. Like snoring. Yes, the sea is snoring, just like Daddy.

"My father used to snore. I wonder if you snore? Or whether I do? Lily never said anything about it. One can't hear oneself snoring. I saw a big bed just now, and I decided not to tell you about it. One can't tell you everything, you know. It would be impossible.... Tell me what you have in your drawers and I will tell you about that hotel. That was silly, wasn't it? I talk as if I was a five-year-old. I *was* five years old when we went to Fiume. That's it, Fiume. There was a big red ship in the port. It was called after the sea: Adria."

Uncle Nicholas lived in Fiume. When we walked past that boat I asked my father: "Are we going on board?" "We shall see," he answered, and kept on talking to mother. They always talk to each other, but not to me. Only sometimes. *She* does not talk to me either. I talk to myself. Perhaps she is asleep.

"Are you asleep?"

She is real clever. She is giving a cough to let me know that she is awake. But still she won't reply. I must have upset her. That's right. I said something unkind to her about working in this small room. She is hurt.

"I'm sorry; I didn't mean to upset you."

"How did you upset me?"

She is a bitch. She really is. Now she is pretending that she wasn't hurt. She wants me to feel so small that I can't even upset her. But don't worry; I shall upset her all right. Bitch! I shan't talk to her now, then she will be real sorry. But I am behaving like a child. Everything I feel and think is childish. I must show her that I am not a child, then she will talk to me. But that is childish too. Pretending that you are a grownup, when you aren't. God, I feel mixed up!

"I feel mixed up."

"Yes, you seem to be angry with me. Why are you angry, Mr. Heimler?"

Mr. Heimler, she said. So she does not consider me a child. Nobody called me Mr. Heimler when I was five years old. They called me Jancsi. Mr. Heimler, she said. I may feel like a child, but I am not a child. That's it. Now I am not so confused. What did she ask?

"I am sorry; I forgot what you asked me."

"Why are you angry with me?"

She didn't say Mr. Heimler that time. Funny woman. One moment she is all right, the next moment she seems very strange. Is she strange, or am I strange? She asked me something just now and I have forgotten again what it was.

"You don't seem to want to remember."

That's it. She is angry with me now ... or just wait a second, she ... that's right, she asked me if I was angry with her. And I think she is angry with me. Am I going mad?

"You somehow manage to make me feel quite small. Oh, I don't know, perhaps it's not your fault, perhaps it's mine. I do feel small. I am small and miserable and lonely. Nobody talks to me. I always have to be nice, because then people will talk to me. If I say 'sorry,' then people talk to me. Sorry, Mummy; sorry, Daddy ... may I kiss you now, Susan? You have to be good to be liked, and if you aren't good, they don't like you I'm sorry I have kept these things back from you ..."

"You seem to be apologizing to me now. You want me to like you. You have tried to make me angry, to try me out. Now you seem to trust me more, because I am not angry with you."

"It makes sense, doctor. It really does. Why haven't I grown up like you have?"

She only answers when she chooses. But she is not like the others ... mother, father and Susan. She knows what she is after. When she does not answer, she wants me to find my own answer. I think I am going to like her quite a lot.

*   *   *

"Last night I had that dream again, doctor. You know, the one I told you about. I was in prison again, and Lily came to see me, but she stayed outside the prison gate. She looked so beautiful, and I was afraid that I might lose her while I was in jail. It wasn't even a proper prison, it was a pit. The light came in through a hole above, and I was quite, quite alone. I tried to reach that opening above me, even though I knew that if I succeeded, guards would be standing there, SS guards, and would shoot me down. But however hard I tried I could not crawl up the wall. I prayed and then I cursed God's name, but it wasn't any use. Then suddenly I realized that after all I wasn't alone. I looked into the darkness, my eyes full of tears, and I saw you coming towards me. You brought a ladder with you, doctor, and we both crawled up it and got out. I looked around to find the guards, but there were none there. I was so grateful to you then, more than I can say. When I woke up, I felt that I wanted to write a poem to you ... I didn't write it, though. After Lily had gone to work, I sat for some time at my desk, but I couldn't write. I felt somehow guilty for wanting to write a poem to you."

"Why guilty, Mr. Heimler?"

"I don't really know. I felt that I was letting someone down. I don't know whom. I don't know why..."

I do know, of course. But how can I tell her? ... Winter evening, dark sky. Rain. Hardly a soul on the streets. Just got out of bed. Tonsillitis, but I feel better now. The fire in the stove crackles cheerfully. Mother is reading a book. "What are you reading, Mummy?" "Listen to this," she says, and puts me on her lap. "A world of its own," she goes on. "Poetry, Jancsi...."

I am five years old, or am I six? I don't understand the words, but her voice is beautiful. The rhythm of the words is also beautiful. There is music in the words, a story about a man who sought happiness. What is happiness? The street is dark outside, but the open door of the stove gives all the light we need. There is sunshine in the valley, and a river, and flowers too. I look at the flames and at mother's face. "I wanted to be an actress, Jancsi," she says, putting down the book. "I love poetry, my little boy." I love poetry, too. It makes Mummy's face shine, like the sun over that river she was talking about. I am a little dazed. "Mummy, please read some more." I feel a slight throbbing in my head. The room turns gently round, and round again. I only hear the music of her voice. "Are we happy, Mummy, you and I?" She laughs. There are bells in her throat. "Of course we are." Then she tells me about her secret wish. I sit up. "What is it, Mummy, what is it?"

"Once upon a time, before you were born" – the words swing in circles – "I wished to have a little boy. You see, we had Susan then, and Daddy and I said one night ... we ought to have a little villain in the house. But it was eight years after Susan's birth before you appeared, you monkey-face." I am not really a monkey-face... "Now, just before you were born in March, I said to Daddy: 'Ernest, I always wanted to have a son more than anything else,' and your father said: 'Maria, this is not quite true, you wanted to be an actress more than anything else.' 'True, true,' I said to Daddy then, 'but I became your wife and I had to give up my dreams. Now, Ernest, what if our son, if it is a boy, should become a poet, who writes poems for actresses to recite?' And Daddy said that it would be very nice, he would like that too. That was our secret wish that night, Daddy's and mine. One day, perhaps, if the good Lord helps you to become a man, you may become a poet, and then however old I may be, I shall recite your poems to your children on a cold night like this. And I shall be with you when pretty actresses recite the words you wrote. I shall be with you always when you write."

"My mother wanted me to become a poet when I was a child. I sat on her lap one winter evening, and she told me that this was her secret wish..."

"And you don't want to let your mother down? You don't want to share that secret with me?"

She knows. She knows more about me than I know myself. Does she know that when I was nine years old, and mother was lying in bed with the illness that killed her in the end ... what was it, now? Pernicious anemia? ... and I was at home from school for the holidays, I was frightened that she might die, and sat down to write the first poem of my life? It was about a just king of Hungary, King Matthias. I waited until she woke, then I sat on her bed and read to her. "It's beautiful, Jancsi ... you are a poet all right...."

Does she know that when I was fourteen years old, I sat one winter night alone in my little room while doctors fought for mother's life, and a specialist was on the way from Buda-

MY LIFE AFTER AUSCHWITZ

pest ... does she know that rain was falling outside, and the stove was warm and spluttering cheerfully ... does she know that I looked up at the sky and remembered that winter night long ago when she shared her secret with me – and that I sat down then and wrote a poem for her? Does she know, this clever doctor of mine, that while I wrote, my tears fell on the ink ... the past was gone, and the good old days ... and mother might die ... tonight ... tomorrow ... or in a year's time? Before the specialist came next day, I read this poem to her, and said: "You promised me once that you would recite my poems one day ..." And to my father's surprise, she sat up in bed with tears in her eyes and recited the poem to us. I knew then that I should have to write, write a lot, to make her well. But she died when I was seventeen.

"You see, she was so happy when I wrote something. Ever since she died I always feel her presence when I have the pen in my hand."

"You don't want to let her down."

What she means ... oh God, what she means is that throughout these years I have been living with a ghost, that I have not allowed anyone to take mother's place. What she means is that I was so much attached to her, that I have been living a long secret winter night with her ... I have lived with her night and day, sitting in her lap long after she died ... I sat in her lap in Germany, and when I came back I never forgave her that *she* let me down, that she allowed Hitler, the Gestapo, the camps ... oh, dear, dear God ... I couldn't write because I felt let down ... I only started to write when I found her in Lily again ... not Lily for her own sake, but for a past shadow...

"Doctor, I think I am going to cry..."

*   *   *

"Nothing makes sense any more. The world is a cruel place, and I don't understand it. My words are all lies. I don't really lie to you, but all the time I feel as if I was lying to you. And lying to myself. I don't understand anything, anything at all. All the things I have told you are lies, and yet they are not. I feel confused, I feel weak, I feel as if I had committed an awful crime … I must have done something terrible, otherwise God would not punish me like this. I read somewhere that Freud says that God is a father figure. So I may be talking rot, or perhaps not about God at all."

"That is quite possible…"

"You don't tell me, doctor, that you believe in that bull****? I am sorry to be angry, but it is all such nonsense. 'Father figure' indeed! There is a lot of rubbish in this psychogame. There are times when I feel I ought to stop coming here. What have I learned so far? Nothing of any importance."

You are lying again. You know bloody well that you have learned a lot. Why do you say "You" and not "I" …? Oh, go to hell. What a miserable creature you are! Here you lie on this bloody couch and you lie.… That's a good one. You lie and lie.… Nonsense. Everything is nonsense. Why do you go on living, eh? What are you living your wretched life for? What else are you going to find out? In the end you won't even see colors any more. That's right. In the end you will be full of dry rot, like she is. Because she is … and you are … Where has "I" gone today? Where is "I"… let's ask her where it is?

She sits there like a goddess. What a frustrated old so-and-so she must be. Why are you talking to her? Eh? She would like to know the juicy bits of your life, I bet … Now, don't be vulgar. Why not? You won't talk to her today, I can see that. There, there is "I" … I never knew I was mad. Does

everyone who has an analysis go mad like me? Where is "you" now? I have had enough of this. I shall go home ...
"I want to go home now."

* * *

"I am sorry about yesterday, doctor. I don't know what came over me. Please forgive me ... I am frightened of this analysis. I am afraid that in the end I shall be so thoroughly analyzed that I shan't be able to write."
"You mean, that this analysis is a kind of punishment?"
"Well, it is connected somehow with what I felt yesterday. Why should I feel that I am going to be punished?"
"Well, why?"
"Can't you once, only once, give me a proper answer, please? Do you always have to leave the dirty work to me?"
"Why dirty work?"
I don't know why, but this question of hers makes me very uneasy. I said "dirty work" ... what does this have to do with spies? What does it all mean? It has to do with spies, with being watched all the time ... with the SS, the MI5, the Communists ... and, God forgive me, with father ... But I loved you, old man. I really did.... You must believe me.... What did I say yesterday? You are lying again....
"I feel mixed up again about spies and lots of things and..."
"Yes, Mr. Heimler...?"
"Oh, it's ridiculous!"
"Tell me, please?"
She knows I don't want to talk to her about him. She knows everything. I could ... could what, you bastard? I could kill her....
"I didn't tell you yesterday, that I was mixed up by the "I" and the "You" ... I didn't tell you, that "You" talked nasty things to me..."

"What does it say *now*?"

How does she do it? How does she dare to insinuate, that I have any but the most loving feelings towards my old man? Hey ... you ... he is dead.... Ah, so he is....

"I would like to hear about it, Mr. Heimler...."

"Help me. Please help me. I can't do it alone."

"I will help you. There, we shall face it together."

"I can't, doctor ... I can't. ... I am a bastard ... a coward ... a murderer...."

Murderer? Do you remember, when you denied this? Do you remember? After Kato had been raped, on top of the train. You remember what she said: "You coward, you bastard, you stood there watching what happened without a murmur, without an attempt to save me. You are not a man, you are an animal." And then, when you felt guilty and wanted to touch her hair, what did she say? "Murderer? I am no murderer, Kato." Now in heaven's name, what is this all about?

Was it before or after the "secret" incident with mother? Who knows? Perhaps before, perhaps after. I woke one night ... go on. ... I woke one night and ... Go on, you bastard. ... I heard what they did there.... Who, you coward? Mother and father, of course. What did they do?

"Doctor, I want some water, I feel sick."

"Thank you, doctor ... *they* did something terrible in there, in their bedroom.... I woke up frightened, I heard everything.... The Russians did that to Kato...."

"What do you mean?"

"I opened the door quietly.... I saw it all.... He was going to kill her.... I knew it.... He ... the..."

"All right, Mr. Heimler, I am still here...."

"Then he looked at me; there was hate in his eyes. He..."

I can't tell her everything.... I can't. When mother died I was heart-broken, but when I saw him crying ... Oh God....

God, forgive me.... Please, please God, forgive me.... I was glad.... I was glad that he did not have her any more.... You must tell her, Jancsi ... everything will be all right if you tell her....

"Doctor ... Doctor ... when mother died ... he stood by the bed and put on the tefillin, the ceremonial symbols with which he prayed every morning, and cried into her dead ears: 'Hear, O Israel, Our God, Our Lord Our God is One....' He stood there, and we all cried with him ... then ... when I saw his unhappiness ... I felt ... that it served him right ... because..."

"Because you did not want to share your mother with him...."

"Yes ... yes ... yes ... and, doctor ... please, please listen and forgive ... and when the Gestapo took him away I was terribly upset ... and yet I felt as if a great shadow had been lifted off my shoulders.... Please forgive me.... Oh forgive me, please...."

"But you loved him too...."

"Oh, yes ... I loved him with all my heart, and yet I always remembered ... what he did to her...."

"What he did, Mr. Heimler ... he loved your mother ... like you did."

He loved her too.... Strange, that never occurred to me until now. Not really, not the way I understand him *now*.... Of course he loved her ... Of course he did ... and I loved her too, and him. Why in heaven's name didn't I know this before? Why did I have to go through life believing that he wanted to kill her that night?

"Tears do not make one less of a man, Mr. Heimler."

"Thank you, doctor. Thank you very much."

* * *

Tears do not make one less of a man, but there are times when one has to come face to face with one's persecutor, through tears, through pain, through suffering. There are moments in a man's life when he has to understand that he stopped time a long time ago, at a moment which has remained unchanged by future time. If, in those moments which become crystallized, a man conceives a false idea of the world ... the false idea becomes crystallized too, enveloped in that unmoving time. So it happens that this strange remnant of a past distorts one's picture of the world. Father did not attack mother, but loved her, yet ... I saw only murder on that night. And because there was murder in my heart, too, I sought my punishment through spies and communists and Nazis. The bubble had now burst ... only one of many, it is true, but an important one. When a bubble bursts in the mind, the past remains in the past; it will not reach into the present, nor will it destroy tomorrow.

* * *

My analysis came to an end in December, and I said goodbye to my doctor. She had represented for me many important figures of my past. Through her I had relieved and experienced the thoughts and emotions of bygone years. I called her "doctor," but in fact I had never regarded her as a human being. I had looked upon her as "the goddess," never realizing that she had her own feelings and her own problems. Now when the moment of departure came I suddenly saw her as a human being in her own right, and I felt that she liked me, and that she was sorry for me to leave, and glad too, because her job was finished.

A last look at the little room, the couch, the window, Freud's portrait on the wall ... a last thank-you ... then the stairs and the street ... and the future....

BOOK TWO

NO MAN IS AN ISLAND

MY LIFE AFTER AUSCHWITZ

CHAPTER ONE

As I left you behind in your consulting-room it was as if something had died. Yet something also was born anew at that moment. I remember I stood in the street watching the traffic as if I were seeing it for the first time. I want you to know how I felt, because that beginning was the foundation of my todays. The world looked wan, the red buses looked less red, and the winter sunshine appeared sickly pale. I found myself noticing things that I had hardly noticed before. People's faces, for example; unsmiling, their eyes reflecting a new sadness. They passed by, each rushing towards his own destination, each carrying a weight and trying at the same time to throw it off. Was this part of the reality that we had so often talked about, or was this a part of my own reality? I stood for some time unable to move, wondering how my life would seem without you. While waiting for the bus I had a feeling that you were dead, and yet I knew, thank God, that you were alive. And as I traveled towards the post office where I was doing some temporary work, I realized that I had known this feeling before, when my mother died and we came back from the funeral.

You stood with me by the invisible graves of my father and my sister. I thank you for helping me to bury them. There is nothing more frightening than having a vague knowledge of the death of beloved ones and yet not being able to weep over their graves. You helped me to bury my dead, and yet they remained alive in you. And for that reason I felt that you were both dead and alive yourself.

Through you I have grown, as you have grown no doubt through others. I wanted now that others should be able to grow through me, so that in turn others whom I should never see might grow through them. The visible part of invisible life is the influence of men on men. "No man is an island, entire of itself…"

*   *   *

I always wanted two things in life: to be a psychologist and to become a writer. But wishes do not make reality, nor do gifts; reality is born out of sweat, hard work and tears. I was clear as to my goal, but I did not know yet which road I had to follow to arrive at it.

I envied you, you know. You were a doctor of medicine, a person fully trained to be a pioneer in your chosen field. But the building of my career had been crushed before I had had the chance to choose my profession. Now I was twenty-nine, and it was too late to start at the beginning. I did not have time to study medicine, and then study again for a postgraduate degree, though I would have like to do so. I had to confront the facts of my training so far and my possible abilities, and attach these to something that I could achieve within a reasonable time. Medicine was out. Some branch of psychology perhaps? But which?

You remember we talked about the new profession of psychiatric social work, that you said had great possibilities? I made inquiries about it now, and found that my previous education was acceptable for training in this field. Within a month I was a trainee in a large mental hospital in Kent, and for the first time in my life I was able to face the world of the mentally ill on the other side of the fence.

But after what I had gone through, I realized that there is no such thing as the "other side." Through my experience of suffering I had learned that every man carries within himself both worlds; that the fence is not between oneself and the insane, but between one's own healthy part and the unhealthy.

MY LIFE AFTER AUSCHWITZ

I was afraid in that hospital. I was afraid of the echoing corridors at night, as if madness lurked in the dark corners, and evil spirits walked through the dark buildings, as they did in the beginning of time through the jungle. The primitive and chaotic, the infant in me, sensed dangers where there were none, without realizing that the only danger exists within oneself.

But as time went by I was no more afraid. The voices that my unfortunate patients heard were not mysterious communications from distant planets; they were the voices of the mind, real to them, but unreal to me.

I was seven years old when psychiatric social work started in Britain; when the first Mental Health Course initiated training in a new sphere of social work. I was playing with guns at that time, and breaking Susan's dolls. And probably on the very day that the first students of psychiatric social work were sitting down at their desks, I also was sitting at my desk as a small child, not knowing that my own fate was taking shape.

* * *

The hospital consisted of large buildings, with long, echoing corridors and big, unfriendly wards, where the paint was peeling off the walls. There were more than two thousand patients here, and the medical and nursing staff was quite inadequate to look after them. I arrived at a time of change, when new attitudes were slowly replacing old ones and ignorance was giving way to a new insight.

I learned a great deal in the next eighteen months. I learned how to take a "social history," and how to help patients in their social rehabilitation. It was in the field of rehabilitation that psychiatric social workers could make their particular contribution.

I soon saw that mental illness was not a total blindness of the mind; that there were healthy areas in the minds of the mentally ill that could function with help. I also found that because of this fact many patients, although still ill, could become useful members of society. But to find a job for these men and women did not only mean getting them off the hook, it had to be done with care, with full knowledge of the problems of the patients and of what the world outside could offer them.

The world outside.... A hundred years ago that world saw nothing but evil in the mentally ill; and a few hundred years ago they were burnt at the stake. During the last century "lunatics" were kept away from human habitation, segregated from the world in order not to remind the world of its own insanity. But these "asylums" that were placed apart like leper colonies were slowly surrounded by rows of semidetached houses, until in the middle of the twentieth century the community moved to the door of the mental hospital. When it became possible for men and women to look through their lace curtains across the street and see that beyond the walls of the mental hospital there lives an organized world, fear of it slowly began to die down. But it is still the attitude of the world outside the high walls that determines the fate of its fellow men inside. When that world realizes that mental disease is not a total dictatorship over man, then many more may be able to cross those barriers, until one day the need for them may disappear altogether.

* * *

You helped me to find my place in the world, doctor, and you also helped me to find Lily afresh.

During my training we lived in a bungalow in the hospital grounds. Lily still went to London to work. But soon that was to finish, because she carried a new life under her heart.

MY LIFE AFTER AUSCHWITZ

Almost the first I knew of it was when the greengrocer, one Saturday morning in August, gave me a large wink between the cabbages and potatoes as if we were both members of the same conspiracy. Then some female nurses threw me strange smiles, and the tobacconist opposite the big gate grinned as he handed over my cigarettes and said: "Well done." But by October, I seemed to have faded out of the picture as a partner in this enterprise of ours. At times it seemed as if I were not even a shareholder any more.

I will never forget that night, November 10, 1951. An ambulance races towards London. The nurse in the ambulance is kind. Seeing my pale face and trembling lips, she orders Lily to sit up while she advises me to lie down – as if I am the bearer of that new life. Everyone is encouraging. Lily says: "Never mind, darling, it will soon be over."

When we arrive at the maternity hospital, the kind nurse changes her benevolent attitude towards me; and when I ask her if I can do anything to help, she looks at me with cold, despising eyes. "Yes," she says, "you can pray."

* * *

After the misery of that unforgettable night, I telephoned the hospital in the morning, to be told that Lily had delivered a healthy baby boy.

I carefully chose an expensive bouquet of Lily's favorite flowers, and prepared a short but affecting speech with which to greet her. As visiting time drew near, I almost wept for joy; and on my way to the hospital, I pictured our joyous greeting, my grateful, tender kiss, and the happiness on her face for having accomplished the man-child she wanted.

I arrived too early, but after one look at my face the liftboy without a word deposited me outside the maternity ward. In the waiting room the fathers sat in a group. I gave them a warm smile, but it passed unnoticed. The leader of the group was a large bull-necked man of about forty who, I gathered, had become the father of a nine-pound baby girl a few days previously, his third child. "The baby," he declared to the junior crowd, "will be put on the bottle." I noticed that I was the only one carrying flowers, and quickly concluded that all the others must have been established and recognized fathers for several days, if one only took flowers on the first day.

Eager to learn from my seniors, I asked Bull-neck if he thought bottle feeding was equal to breast feeding. I had asked the wrong thing. He came over to me with a look in his eyes that made me lay the flowers on the seat beside me, and stopped in front of me, looking immense, like those stone gods in the desert. "I am a bottle-fed baby myself," he ejaculated.

"Well, that's proof indeed," I whispered, grateful that he did not desire to demonstrate what strength a bottle-fed baby may gather on the way.

Sister's voice saved me from the bottle-fed, as she shouted: "Faaathers..."

This was the moment of entry into paradise. Holding hard to the last remnants of dignity, I managed not to run. I sensed that something was missing, but what? What was not in my hand that should have been? My God! The flowers! I raced back to the waiting-room. They had gone. I felt very disappointed. What would she think of my miserliness in not bringing her flowers on this important day? Then I thought: "Flowers ... what are flowers? It's me she wants ... the father of her child ..." and with head held high, I walked back to the ward.

I gently kissed her lips. "Darling," I started, but she interrupted me.

"Jancsi," she whispered, "didn't you bring any flowers? You know that I don't care personally, but the sister ... she's such a so-and-so ... and she doesn't like husbands..."

"She doesn't have to," I replied angrily.

I was just about to tell her that my flowers had disappeared from the waiting-room, when she interrupted me. "Look at that man over there ... sister likes him ... he brings flowers to his wife every day."

I looked at the fortunate "Sister's choice," to recognize Bull-neck, handing over *my* flowers to his wife.

"Those are my flowers," I told her in alarm. "Shall I ask for them back?"

"Oh, don't be ridiculous, Jancsi..."

Moments passed by. I felt angry with the entire world. Then Lily asked me to lean towards her.

"Never again, Jancsi," she whispered into my ear, "never again."

"Never again, what?" Vaguely, I still had the flowers in mind. But after looking at her face, I realized the full meaning of her words.

"Never again do I want to go through all that..."

I left the hospital a very disappointed man. The baby looked like a Chinese. "Jaundice," explained the nurse. Lily had said: "Never again." And the porter said at the gate of my own hospital: "You don't look well, Mr. Heimler. What's the matter?"

*   *   *

I wanted to share all these things with you, doctor, because for some time you continued to be a part of my life. The process of breaking away from you altogether was rather a slow one. Whenever anything happened, good or bad, I wondered what you would say about it, what you would advise me to do, how you would react. The time was not very far off when I should see you as separate from, and not as a part of me. But as yet that moment had not arrived.

MY LIFE AFTER AUSCHWITZ

What happened next was one of the greatest trials of my life. I don't think I exaggerate. Until now, I had always been excluded from the rest of humanity by reason of the fact that I was born a Jew. But now the moment came when I was excluded for a different reason: because I was *me*.

After spending a year as a trainee in the mental hospital, I had to apply to the Mental Health Course for my final training to become a psychiatric social worker. The hospital authorities had stated they were satisfied that after qualification I should be able to do the work required of me. Then a letter arrived on March 14, 1952

The letter informed me that the Selection Committee had decided that it was not possible to offer me a vacancy in the Mental Health Course. The writer, who was one of the tutors of the Course, went on to say that she realized I would be very disappointed about the decision, although she expected that I had been partly prepared for it. She assured me that much time and very careful consideration had been given to my application before the decision was made. Finally, she added that she did not think there would be any point in my making a further application, because the Committee was unlikely to view my application differently at a later date.

Before I received this letter I had already attended several interviews. It seemed, however, that the selectors had not been completely certain about my stability, because they requested me to attend yet another interview. It was this one that finally made them decide not to accept me.

As soon as I entered the interviewer's consulting room, I felt that there was something wrong. I never like it if people sit behind a desk, as if to separate themselves from others.

That middle-aged man sitting behind his desk at that moment represented to me all the force of authority which had caused me so much pain in the past. I must describe the details of this interview in all fairness to the interviewer, be-

MY LIFE AFTER AUSCHWITZ

cause it was I who saw him in that authoritarian role, and my interpretation of what he meant was not necessarily his. I resented, moreover, the fact that it was this man who could decide my fate. My resentment was even greater because I felt that my previous interviewers had not taken into consideration the painful realities of my past. In seeking out the weaknesses of my personality, which were only too obvious, they had thought that everything I was, was the result of inner mental conflict, that mind and the world outside the mind had a close relationship. That persecution to me was real and not a delusion alone, they could not see. I resented this because I expected the teachers of an important profession to know more, to understand more, particularly if they called themselves psychiatric social workers. Within myself I was already attacking him for things he was not responsible for.

There were two chairs in front of his desk, an easy chair and a hard one. I thought he was watching me, to see which one I was going to take. Again because I could not grasp the symbolic significance of the chairs, because I sensed that every move I made was to decide the future of my life, I resented him even more. And yet he had not spoken a word so far.

Eventually, I chose the easy chair, and then he spoke:

"Why do you want to become a psychiatric social worker?"

How many times had this been put to me! They had asked this question when I became a trainee; they asked the same question in the hospital where I worked; the previous interviewers had asked me the same thing. What can one reply? How can one give an answer that is both true and acceptable? The truth has so many sides to it. I said:

"The first time I became interested in the mentally ill was during the war, after the Germans invaded Hungary. My father was arrested then and I had to escape to save my skin. The Physician Superintendent of our local mental hospital, a decent man, gave me shelter for some time. It was there that I first met the mentally ill, not in the role of a patient, but in that of a refugee."

For some moments there was silence, and then he said: "Oh, yes." This meant that he wanted to know more.

"You see," I went on, "that was an unusual situation to be in. Those patients were persecuted by the forces of their own minds, and I was persecuted by my enemies. I could somehow identify myself with them, and at the same time feel pity for them, because I knew that if I survived one day my agonies would come to an end, while they would continue to face their private darkness even when I was free."

I sensed again that he did not approve of what I had said; and that he felt I was being superficial and dealing in generalities He said again:

"Oh, yes."

The fact that I was being treated like a patient without having chosen him as my therapist, and that I was being asked to reveal my intimate thoughts to a stranger, was most repugnant to me at that moment. Had he said more, had he been able to forget the respective roles we played and to bridge the desk with interest and warmth, I would not have felt so desperate. My anger grew as I concluded that a wrong interpretation had been put on what I had said.

"I had an analysis," I went on, "because I felt impotent, because I had dried up and couldn't write, because I wanted to overcome the tragedies of my life. I have now faced myself and realized that the no-man's-land between my sanity and insanity is not as great as I thought before my analysis. I feel now that I can understand my patients better because we share something in common...."

"What do you mean?"

"I mean that the motivation behind my wish to become a PSW is the knowledge of my own inferno…"

"Perhaps you are too keen to prove that you are not impotent...."

I sensed that the die was cast, and that he had found confirmation of my instability. I tried to make a last desperate effort to change his mind about me.

"I feel that I can do this work, provided I am given the chance. Please support my application." And when he did not reply, I asked him straight out:

"Will you support my application?"

He replied evasively that he did not know; it was not up to him to decide.

* * *

Today, when I reflect on those events of the past I do not blame anyone. The impression I gave then must have been proof of my inability to cope with my emotions. Those who interviewed me sensed rebellion behind my words, and they were right. But I was rebelling not against them, but against an insane world that has created a vast zoo in which, behind the bars of their cages, behind national frontiers, men are separated from men. I rebelled against a world in which wild animals eat the helpless ones. I rebelled to defend myself, to show the world that I could take my place in life as well as the next man.

One of the traits of my personality lies in the fact that I am not prepared to accept defeat. This may be a traditional characteristic of the people of my faith; but to accept defeat to me means to accept the rule of the dictator.

The selection committee had made its choice; but I also had made mine. Determined now more than ever to succeed, I applied elsewhere. I was accepted, and in the end I managed to qualify. But my experience with the interviewer left a mark on me; and the mood of rebellion stayed with me for a long time after that.

MY LIFE AFTER AUSCHWITZ

CHAPTER TWO

All this time I was growing slowly away from you, doctor. The need to communicate with you in thought had become less and less. I wanted to feel that I was free of you when I started my first job, so that I could begin without a stone around my neck. I know you will not misunderstand.

* * *

I write these words at a time in my life when I have proved to myself and to the world that there is no defeat. This is my message of hope. If there is no defeat for one man, then there can be no defeat. There are tears, there is sweat, there is pain and struggle, but there is no defeat.

As I close my eyes, pictures appear on the screen of my mind. Pictures of home that have led me to this present moment. The past appears dim, but I can see that after 1953 there was no turning back.

The scene I recall lies under the shadow of Westminster Abbey; the time is October 11, 1953. Big Ben chimes three o'clock as the traffic flows with an even rhythm round Parliament Square.

Beyond the bustle of traffic, behind Guildhall in Old Queen Street, stands an old building, offices of the Middlesex County Council. On the first floor is a nondescript waiting room, with a large, useless table in the middle of it which occupies most of the space. There are some pictures on the wall whose purpose is not quite clear: in one, someone is spraying the inside of an airplane; in another, a miserable child is being vaccinated by a happy doctor. People walk through the waiting room as if I wasn't there: it is more like a corridor than a

MY LIFE AFTER AUSCHWITZ

waiting room. There are doors everywhere. Which one will open for me?
I am waiting for the interview for my first job.
A door opens now and a tall man in his forties appears. He smiles:
"Please come in."
Behind the easy chair where I sit there is a large map of Middlesex. The telephone rings; he covers the mouthpiece with his palm. "You will forgive me for just a moment?" As he speaks on the telephone I observe that he sits behind an enormous desk, covered with papers. His desk lamp shines into my face. Blast it! Buchenwald ... the night when the Gestapo officer turned the headlights on to us and we stood in the falling snow staring into that glaring light. He puts the receiver down. "I am sorry," he says, while he moves from behind his desk to the other easy chair facing me. Why do I think of the chestnut trees in our garden in Savaria? He walks with slow, deliberate movements. He forgets his pipe. He walks back to the desk again, unhurried: there is plenty of time. There were conkers on the ground then. There are no conkers in Parliament Square. He sits down: "What an awful summer we've had; and the autumn is even worse." I want to say: "Sir, please, sir, there are no chestnut trees in front of your window." I must be mad.

"This is an informal interview, you understand. You will have to attend another one, of course, with the Chairman and other committee members...." Has the Chairman got a moustache? Father had one – and he was a County Councilor, too. How would it go if he should interview me, from beyond the grave?

"As you know, there are no traditions in Community Care. We have had one or two PSWs, but no pattern has been established as yet. I'm sure that is better for everyone concerned, for it means you will be able to find your own particular interest in the field, develop your own methods."

I follow his words. My world is taking shape. But what is that fly doing there, in the middle of October too? I have a desire to say: "Dr. Wigley, there is a fly over there. Can't you get hold of one of those sprayers of yours?"

"I will assist you in every way I can. Community Care is only an infant today, but it will grow to maturity in time."

Father once wrote to me that one's station in life is improved if one can live among intelligent people. This man seems intelligent.

"The future lies with the care of the mentally ill in their own homes. Professor Querido in Amsterdam has proved that this is not entirely impossible."

What will I prove? What will my share be in this new concept of Community Care? Will someone, somewhere, say one day at an interview similar to this: "Heimler has proved that it was not impossible?"

He speaks slowly in his public school voice:

"The county is divided into five mental health divisions. In each division there are a few Mental Welfare Officers who are duly authorized under the Act and have the power to certify if necessary. Some have had vast experience, but they have had no training.'"

Where is the fly? It has gone, flown out of the top of the open window. It will die ... the fly will die in Parliament Square. The telephone rings again as I say goodbye. Big Ben chimes four o'clock, and the ancient Abbey looks down on the small foreigner who is leaving the interview for his first job.

On December 1, 1953, I started work with the Middlesex County Council.

* * *

MY LIFE AFTER AUSCHWITZ

On March 14, 1952, on the very day that I received that fateful letter of rejection by the Mental Health Course, thirty miles away a man was staggering towards his death. His name was Frank Latham and neither of us knew then that I should be playing an important part in his life, and he in mine.

On the morning I opened that letter and my world had come to a momentary standstill, I looked at the rain that was pouring down from the sky, the same sky that he saw on that day. He left his home that morning and walked across the wet streets without knowing where he was going; when evening came he found himself in Hyde Park, near the Serpentine. A car was parked there without lights, but the street lamp disclosed the silhouette of a couple on the back seat. They embraced, parted, came together again. Their slow rhythmic movements drew him nearer like a magnet: he felt that he had to watch, to know what was going on. He stood like a statue unable to move, with tears choking his throat, aware only that he desired that unknown woman in the car more than anything else in the world. A voice within his brain screamed: "Kill the bastard ... kill him ... and take her ... go on, take her ..."; but behind the voice his mother's soft voice spoke: "Cry, sonny, cry."

Then, as though propelled from without, he moved towards the lights of the West End.

The girl was standing at a doorway in Wardour Street. She was small and dark with big brown eyes. "Would you like a drink, dearie?" He followed her up the stairs, and she stopped every now and then to hold her thigh with her hands as if to support herself. She was very young, but she walked like an old woman. A smell of fish and chips and onions filled the dim staircase, and the sound of jazz music drifted in from a near-by club. He closed his eyes in an attempt not to see, but when he opened them again he could see the wretched creature standing before the mirror half naked. He gave her some money, but as he watched her lying across the bed waiting for his embrace the whiteness of her body disgusted him; he felt sick and he ran out into the night.

The streets and houses all seemed to be moving vertically up and down, and the pavement rushed at him with terrific force. Cars and buses appeared to be defying the laws of gravity. By the embankment the sound of sirens drifted across the wind towards south London … and there it lay – the beautiful dark water under the great pillars of Westminster Bridge, inviting him to a final embrace. Then he jumped…

*   *   *

Frank was my first patient. He telephoned me in December on the advice of the Area Officer of the National Assistance Board.

"If you take a trolley-bus from Finchley Central to Tally Ho Corner, look for Sainsbury's, our building is next to it. Come up to the second floor."

I was alone in my office. It was a small office, with a fair-sized desk and two armchairs facing each other. A small carpet covered the polished floor and reached to Mrs. Niven's typewriter by the window. By the door stood the cabinet in which my future records were to be kept.

I was restless. My first patient was late. Or had he changed his mind? It was raining outside, and I watched the little circles of rain which formed on the windows and ran down the panes like tear-drops before disappearing. I felt a little sad and lonely. Lily and baby George were still up north, in the university town where I had completed my studies, and I had not seen them since I came to London. What were they doing now? In two days' time it would be Christmas and I should go home.

Frank Latham arrived an hour late.

"I walked."
That was all he said. He didn't say "good afternoon" or "sorry I'm late." He just said: "I walked." And yet in the way he said it there was both a greeting and some desperation. He had not only walked, but he was soaked to the skin.
I put the electric fire on. He didn't say "thank you"; he just moved across and stood looking down at it. He was tall, blond, possibly about my age. Suddenly he turned round.
"Well, what can I do for you?"
No one had ever taught me what to answer to that one. This wasn't in the textbook. All the patients I had seen at the hospital and at the university had acted their proper roles. I felt that I had suddenly fallen out of my own role, too; but I covered up.
"Would you like to sit down?" I asked, not being able to think of anything better.
"No," he said. "I don't want to sit down, do you mind?"
But he sat down all the same. He sat down on the edge of my desk. I had never seen any patient sitting on the edge of my teacher's desk, and I felt anger rising in me. How dare he behave like this! And my first patient, too! I was just going to say something to this effect, when suddenly I realized that my new patient was *acting* out what he could not or did not want to say. I tried to translate what all this meant, and then I understood what he was not saying: "Don't you see, I couldn't care less about anything. I am fed up with you, with myself, with the bloody National Assistance Board. They think you can help me; well, I'll prove to you that you can't. I shall annoy you so much that in the end you will throw me out, you bastard 'trick cyclist.'"
I answered his unspoken words aloud:
"You are wrong, you know. I am not going to throw you out."

He did not even notice that I had been answering his thoughts.

"You'll get fed up with me, you'll see."

He stood up and put a foot on the arm of the easy chair in order to tie his shoelaces.

At that moment I felt sorry for him.

"I am sorry that you don't like me," I said.

"I don't dislike you," he answered, looking into my eyes. "I just think you are nuts. Nobody can help me, nobody."

Then he walked to the door and disappeared without saying another word.

* * *

Frank Latham came back early in the New Year without an appointment. This time he didn't even knock on the door.

"Well how are you today?" was his greeting, "I hope you feel better now...."

I said I was feeling much better, thanks. He walked over to the window and just stood there for several minutes without saying anything.

Mrs. Niven got up to prepare some tea.

He looked at the typewriter, and glanced at the letter my typist had left in it.

"I see you are busy now?"

I said I was, but that we could arrange an appointment for another day.

Frank did not answer my suggestion, but said, looking at the ceiling:

"This bloody place needs redecorating. I might do it for you one of these days."

I repeated: "Would you like to come to see me when I am free?"

"Okay, if I remember."

He walked out again without another word, and as he walked down the stairs he was whistling a popular tune.

A month later he turned up unexpectedly; I found him waiting for me when I arrived at my office. He was pale with black rings under his eyes, his blond hair was unkempt, and he badly needed a shave. He sat looking blankly ahead, and when he spoke there was no arrogance, neither in his words and movements, nor in the tone of his voice. He said:

"Some people should never have been born. Some people should have rotted away before they came into this lousy world."

Suddenly the words of Job came into my mind. *"Why died I not from the womb? Why did I not give up the ghost when I came out of the belly?"*

Frank got up and went to the window, tears flowing down his cheeks, and I did not disturb his silent weeping. Then after a while, his face smeared with tears, the dam burst and his story unfolded.

* * *

During the next few weeks I learned what lay behind Frank Latham's unhappiness. To the National Assistance Board he was "work-shy," a man who in the past seven years had never kept a job for longer than a week. To them he presented a façade of arrogance, of not caring. To me he now presented another picture. His story started thirty years ago in Moss Side, Manchester. He did not remember much of his very early years, for pain had erected strong barricades against memory. He did, however, remember a night when, as a small boy, he had woken in terror in the middle of the night to find his mother bleeding from a flesh wound his father had inflicted on her. It must have been a summer night, because small creepy things were flying round the electric bulb. The bulb swayed from the ceiling, and light and shadow danced dizzily in the kitchen. He never remembered his father's face, or his voice. Nor did he understand at that time what his father had done, or why. He did not even know it today. He remembered the ambulance and crying bitterly when they took his mother to the hospital. Then there was a long blank, filled only with the faces of other men with whom his mother had lived. Never in his life had he uttered the word "father" to anyone. He remembered the bedroom of the orphanage, and the nuns switching off the light. Why his mother had put him into an orphanage he also did not know, but now he was ashamed for her sake at what she had done. He was good at his studies and he matriculated; and just before the war he learned bookkeeping. Then as if in a nightmare he remembered flying above the burning German towns. What was he doing on that airplane? Was he the navigator? He could not remember. One day in 1944 he was taken to hospital because of a sudden attack of appendicitis. That night his plane and all his comrades were shot down over Hamburg and the whole crew was lost; and an agony started for him that he could not put into words. He felt responsible for the death of the others, and no "trick cyclist" was able to convince him that he was not.

Frank was demobbed in 1945 with what the doctors called neurasthenia. Somehow or other he managed to go through the summer doing odd jobs, washing up at the Corner House, helping a decorator for a few days, but when autumn came bad dreams began, and even cigarettes tasted bitter. It would have been nice to go home, but there was no home to go to: his mother had died in the blitz. During his haunted nights he would stare into the corners of his rented room, where hundreds of devils were hidden behind the big wardrobe. With morning came voices that shouted in his head and threatened him with death. Then he would go through the damp streets, frightened of the cold unfriendly houses whose blind windows peered down at him, while the voices drove him on, farther and farther, towards the unknown.

But somehow he staggered through the years, like a shadow in a dark night. He married in 1948, and for a while everything was fine. He felt that if God offered him no salvation, Evelyn could. But a month after their marriage, Frank was suddenly overcome by a vast restlessness. He tried to find consolation in a Soho club.

There were many of these little basement clubs in Soho, ill lit, crowded, with hardly any furniture, where lost human beings seek relief from conflicts through the pleasures of the flesh. Here, beyond the sweaty faces and the laughter that is stimulated by alcohol and drugs, is a world of fear and death. Years pass swiftly here ... and the years passed over Frank like heavy clouds across a winter sky. At first he still lived with Evelyn, who watched his unhappiness in bewilderment, but when their little daughter was born in early 1952 he moved away from home. Down in the belly of the earth an artificial sun was shining in "Adam's Leaf," and Frank believed that the light he saw was the light of the living sun. But on March 14 he wanted to end it all. That was the night he jumped into the Thames.

He was taken to a mental hospital, where he fell into a seemingly endless darkness, into the echo of a limitless tunnel, into a pool of unrecognizable memories. Six times he awoke exhausted with a sick feeling in his stomach, unable to remember present or past.

But after the six electric shock treatments, the grief and confusion receded. He no longer felt like a soul lost in a nightmare, but a man who had to shave, drink his tea, wash himself and do something with his life.

After he left hospital he returned home to his wife and child. But he could not settle down, and the months passed like a day, with no aim, no purpose, no hope. And now he was with me, begging for help. But help for what?

*   *   *

I asked myself during the long winter evenings what ought to be my function, what was my proper role? I was no psychoanalyst trained to treat the mind by the method *she* used. (You see, doctor, how the umbilical cord that connected me to you has now been cut!) I was not trained in medicine to give medical relief through drugs or other chemical means. I had to discover my own methods if I was to help Frank. But how?

It was a very experienced colleague of mine who had worked for many years in the field of Community Care who helped to clarify my mind.

"You may think, perhaps," she said to me, sitting in my office, "that to limit one's aims indicates inferior work. But it doesn't, you know. It is in the ability to do this that the possibility of professional growth really lies. The trouble is that we tend to imitate psychiatrists and analysts, perhaps because we would have liked ourselves to become psychotherapists. But we may have a job to do that in the final analysis the others cannot do. The crux of the matter is to develop our own skills by focusing our attention on what we *can* do."

"My difficulty," I confessed to her, "is that I am not certain what I *can* do. Here is a man who is begging me for help, presenting me with his problem, and I am not at all sure what to do with all that material."

"Among the many things that he presents to you," she said thoughtfully, "he shows you his inability to take his place in society, among ordinary men and women. He is unable to keep his family, or for that matter to keep himself. Don't you think that this is the area within which you will have to work?"

"All right, then. How am I going to help him to take his place in the world when he's too blocked emotionally to be able to make the first step? It's a vicious circle, you know. He cannot work, because he is emotionally disturbed, and he cannot be helped to work until he becomes emotionally stable."

"Then you will have to help him to the point of emotional stability where he will be able to work again."

"What you are in fact saying," I replied, "is that a certain amount of psychotherapy will be necessary after all."

"Oh yes, indeed, but your aim will not be to remove his symptoms or cure his sickness, but to focus on his social rehabilitation. Once your own aims are clear, you may find that the methods you have to use will be different from those of orthodox psychotherapy."

*   *   *

One day towards the end of March, Frank asked me if I would care to go for a walk with him in Friary Park. I remembered then his attitude when he first came to see me, how he had declined to sit on the chair but had instead sat on the edge of my desk, and how, although at subsequent interviews he had seemed much happier; there had always been some uneasiness on his part in conforming. There was something in the way he looked at me now that made me feel as if this request for a walk was really important to him: it was almost as if he wanted to test me out to see if I were willing to go with him.

I had been trained to remain outside a patient's life and problems, and had always been told by my teachers at the university that the therapeutic relationship must not be a social one; that I might be friendly towards my patients, but should never become their friend. I saw clearly the wisdom of this teaching. It was the very fact that he was an outsider that enabled the social worker to sort out the social and emotional problems of a patient. The environment of the office or consulting-room was also a kind of defense against this involvement, and by reminding him all the time that he was there to help, it helped the social worker in many ways.

The problem I had to face now was whether a professional relationship could be maintained if I gave up the security of my office and entered a semi-social relationship with Frank. Would I be able to use a "social" situation to help him? Or were my teachers right in saying that I would eventually be so involved with him that I could not help him at all? Yet the coin had another side. The very fact that he had asked me to go for a walk indicated that he trusted me, and wanted me to become his friend. I knew from what he had told me so far that one of the great difficulties of his life was his failure to establish relationships with others. Was this not my opportunity to help him to do this by proving to him that he was wanted?

What was I here for, anyway? If I was called a Community Psychiatric Social Worker, did this not mean that I must cope with my patients' problems within the structure of society, away from hospitals and clinics? Was it not possible that my teachers based their own techniques on hospital and clinical practices merely because they were used to them? If I was a social worker, did this not mean that I must follow the traditions of the pioneers of social work, who certainly had no hesitation in sharing the social life of those they were trying to help?

Frank sat in the armchair and looked at me questioningly as these thoughts raced through my mind. What was behind his invitation? Was his motive a positive one? Was he asking me to join him outside the office because he respected and trusted me, or was this an attempt on his part to bring me into

the orbit of his chaotic personal life, and so destroy the possibility of my effective help? I said to him:
"I suppose you would feel happier outside this office?"
He said that he would, and talked about the beauties of spring. But I wondered whether he understood that my willingness to go out with him was to serve a purpose, and that that purpose was to enable him to feel freer to talk to me.
We walked towards Friary Park and for some time we talked very little. But just before we got to the gates he stopped, and said, smiling:
"You're a strange man!"
"Why?"
"I never really thought, you know, that you'd come out with me. I expected you to shake me off just like the others did."
"The others? Which others?"
"When I tried to ... when I ... you know, jumped into the river and was taken to that hospital, everyone treated me as if I was insane, as if I was mentally ill."
"But you *were* mentally ill," I said.
"You don't seem to understand what I mean. Of course I was crazy, I know that, but they shouldn't have treated me as if I was."
When I did not reply, he stopped walking and said with feeling:
"I'll try to explain. After I was taken to that hospital, the first person I saw next morning was a doctor, a psychiatrist, a tall, thin, nervous-looking man, who never once looked me in the face. We sat in his consulting-room at the Admission Villa, with my case papers in front of him. There was nothing written on those papers yet, except my name. The doctor then proceeded to ask a lot of questions, trying to find out what had led to my breakdown. 'When did you first notice that something was wrong with you?' 'What sort of illnesses did

you have as a child?' 'Why did you want to take your life?' 'What is your appetite like?' 'How do you sleep?' I answered him as truthfully as I could, hoping all the time, that once, just once, he would raise his eyes from those damned papers and look at me, not as a case, but as a human being. But, no. He just went on asking questions, and the more he asked, the more I was made to feel that I was a failure. And what a failure! His questions brought out my hopeless situation, my madness, but not one was concerned with anything positive in me. Why didn't he say: 'So you are a man who desperately wants to love and be loved.' or 'Tell me, Mr. Latham, about your ambitions in life before your first breakdown, when you were able to work and were in good health.' Had he asked me this kind of question too, or let me know by one glance that he was aware of the good as well as the bad in me, I could have opened up much more. But he wasn't interested in my abilities, only in my disabilities – and ill as I was, I knew that my life so far, however imperfect, had not been wholly negative. By this time I was supplying the answers like a computing machine, and I felt, watching the way he went on filling up all those papers, as if nothing mattered to him but to put down the answers. I felt that as long as he had his answers he was content. Why, I could not help wondering, do people like him choose the profession of psychiatry? Just before he concluded the interview, still not having once looked into my eyes, I noticed something on his tie. He must have had egg for breakfast, and a bit of yolk was smeared on it. This somehow showed that he must be human after all. But is it not shocking, that the remains of his breakfast should remind me of his humanity, and not his eyes or his voice? Do you understand what I mean?"

I understood him all right. I remembered my own interview and I knew exactly what he meant. I also knew that the psychiatrist in the Admission Villa would have had his answers ready to Frank's objections. He would have talked about Frank's resistance, about "transference," and Frank's need to see him in his denying role; he would have been able to supply all the textbook answers to his objections, except to see that his own attitude had something to do with Frank's feelings.

Of course Frank had resisted, and naturally he had wanted to see in that doctor a positive "fatherly" man such as he had never had in his own life. And it is also true that Frank was quick to see in his denial a reflection of his own past tragedy. All this is true, and yet the truth lies not only on one side of the desk.

Frank could talk about this painful episode to me, because I treated him differently. His craving for a positive masculine figure was not only a symptom, but also a reality, and now in me he saw the hope of such a person. He wanted more than questions, or answers, or words. He wanted to be loved, so that eventually he himself could love again.

He led me to a distant part of the park, from where he could see everything without himself being seen. A short way off, children were playing on the roundabouts, while their mothers sat on the benches talking. The children were noisy, happy, carefree, and the park was alive with their voices. He watched the children playing. For some minutes neither of us said anything.

When I had my analysis, there had been times when I saw my analyst as a goddess. At other times she had appeared as mother, or sister, or father. I was able to see her in these roles because she remained aloof, and I did not know anything about her life. I saw in her a mirror of my past and present, according to my fancies and desires. But by the very fact of my being with Frank together in the park, I was not just an image of fantasy. I was a real man, and he could no doubt perceive a great deal of this reality from the way I walked or coughed or smoked my cigarette, or from the way I reacted to what he said. And yet behind this reality, there was also his need for that father he never had. At that moment in Friary Park I believe that I became a bridge for him between reality and fantasy, and I felt that this would probably be my most important contribution to him.

"You have chosen a spot," I pointed out to him, "where you can see others, but where you cannot be seen."

"So I have! That's funny."

"Funny? Why?"

He thought for a few minutes.

"Because this is what I do all the time. I like to see others being happy, but I don't like others to see my unhappiness."

"How would others know you were unhappy even if they saw you?"

A long silence ensued. Then he said:

"I never thought about it, really. I always thought that I had it written all over me."

"But you haven't got it written all over you."

"I must have thought that *they* could read my thoughts."

"But no one can really read your thoughts."

"Well, I must have put *my* thoughts into *their* heads."

"I think that is true, Mr. Latham."

Silence again. I said:

"You sit there in your corner like a sad little boy."

"I feel like a sad little boy," he said. "Look at them"; pointing his fingers towards the children, "they're happy. I was never happy. I never had a mother like those mothers … you know, Mr. H – you don't mind if I call you Mr. H, do you? – you know, Mr. H, I really think … that when I get into a corner like this, I do it … because I envy them, I even hate them … and I don't want them to see how much I really hate them …"

"And perhaps you think that they hate you too?"

"Yes, that's it ... I creep into my corner because I think that they're laughing at me. But that's all nonsense – they don't even notice I exist. Oh, dear me, Mr. H ... it's because I know that they don't even notice me that I go into a corner, so that I can imagine they're mocking me and hating me ... anything is better than not being noticed. Yes, that makes sense. I seem to be putting my own thoughts into these strangers ... how ridiculous ... I must be doing this with lots of people ... the National Assistance Board officers, for example..."

"What about the National Assistance Board?"

"I always feel when I go there on Fridays that they're thinking I'm no bloody good. I think they want me to feel small. So I raise hell."

"What sort of hell?"

"You know..."

"I don't know."

"Well ... when I think that they're trying to make me feel small, I become abusive. I try to make them feel small instead. You see?"

"Yes, I see. But surely, as you said, you are putting your own thoughts into their heads."

"I see that now."

"Why don't you work, Mr. Latham?"

"I don't know."

"Is it that you don't want to know?"

"Look, Mr. Heimler," (not Mr. H this time), "even if I did decide to work, what sort of work would they offer me? Most of the time it would be some rubbish. I could do something better than that."

"What, for example?"

"If I'd had the opportunity, I could have become a professional man, a doctor or an engineer ... but *they*'ve denied me this opportunity."

"Who? The National Assistance Board?"

He was laughing now.

"Yes."

"But it doesn't make sense to me."

"I want the bastards to pay up for what I've lost."

"I see. You want to make someone responsible for your lack of opportunity, and you have chosen the National Assistance Board as your scapegoat."

"Yes, that's it."

He got up, and asked if we could walk a bit. We started off towards the roundabouts, but as soon as we were mingling with the crowd, he wanted to sit down again, this time very near the children and their mothers. Did he realize, I wondered, that this was his first attempt to be part of that happy crowd?

After a few minutes, he said:

"I will tell you something, Mr. H. I'll have to start afresh. I will make an attempt to work again. For your sake."

"For *my* sake?" I asked surprised. "Why for my sake?"

"Because I feel that you disapprove, so I shall try my best."

"But why not for your own sake, or for the sake of your family?"

"It will be for your sake. I am going to prove something to you."

"What?"

"I am going to prove to you that I shall not let you down. I must do it for your sake, because I trust you. I don't trust myself."

He looked round, and said with a sigh:

"Funny, I don't feel so depressed now."

* * *

A week later, when Frank came to see me, he reported that he had started work as a traveler for a North London firm. He suggested that we should celebrate the occasion by going to a nearby pub at Tally Ho Corner.

"Well, what do you think?" he started, after he had ordered our beer. "I'm a working man again."

I said that I was pleased to hear it. We drank, and I noticed that he drank his beer in one gulp, as if he was very thirsty. I commented on this.

"No, I'm not really thirsty. It's a habit."

"You finished that almost as if you were afraid that someone might take it away from you."

He looked round at the other customers cautiously before replying.

"You give them a half a chance, and they *would* take it away from you."

"You can't be serious," I said, smiling. "Don't tell me that any of these people in the pub are after your beer?"

"Children would take anything away from you, if you gave them a chance."

"Children?"

He hesitated.

"Did I say children? I really meant people."

"Why children, Mr. Latham?"

I ordered another couple of beers, and again he drank his even before I could sit down.

"Did I say children? Funny. You see, Mr. H, when I was in that orphanage" – he had both his hands round the empty glass – "the children were always pinching my things. They took my food if I didn't watch out. One morning when I woke up, even my shoelaces had gone, and when I complained to the nuns, they walloped me. Grown-up people are not very different to children."

It was an ordinary pub, with ordinary people sitting around, and had they looked at us they would not have noticed anything strange about us. Even if they could have overheard our conversation, it would not have seemed entirely out of place: a great many secrets are disclosed in an English pub. And yet it was different from an ordinary conversation. The difference lay not in the choice of our words, but in the situation they revealed. These "interviews" in ordinary social settings were helping Frank, not only to open up, but also to relate himself to his environment. Park or pub, one was as good as another, as long as he had some problem in that particular environment.

He repeated:

"Yes Mr. H, grown people are not very different to children."

I slowly drank my beer as he went on:

"I've thought a great deal about you during the past few weeks, particularly since last week. You're OK – but *you* want to take something away from me too."

I looked up, and saw that there was hostility in his eyes as I asked what he meant.

"Why do you want to help me, Mr. Heimler? Why do you want me to work? Is it because you're a good man, or is it because you and the National Assistance Board are working hand in hand to get me off the books? I've thought about it a lot. I cost the State a lot of money, and the taxpayer doesn't like his money wasted on the 'work-shy.' So you cooked up a scheme by which you cunningly worm your way into my heart ... and there you are ... stupid Frank is working again."

"So you mistrust my intentions now?"

I knew that he was determined to put me to the test. I realized it last week in Friary Park when he told me that he would find work for my sake. I knew, too, that, having broken his old pattern, he would resent the fact of wanting to return my trust in him by trusting me. I learnt during my training that love and hate walk hand in hand, and that man must be able to express both if he wants to grow. I learnt the same thing during my analysis, when I found that the hostility I expressed towards my analyst was not a personal hostility, but that I used her to attack through her those I had loved and hated. So Frank's hostility did not come as a surprise to me. But his next words were a shock. He said:

"Money means a great deal to you Jews, doesn't it? You want it all for yourselves, and it breaks your heart to see it wasted on the 'goy.' on the gentile. Money is God to you people."

A cold shiver ran down my spine. "Money is God to you people." Suddenly, in the middle of an English pub, the words of this suffering man brought back to me the past – the ghetto, the yellow star, the smell of burning flesh over Auschwitz, the anonymous graves of my family and people without end. I tried to tell myself that this was but another form of hostility, that it had little to do with me personally, and yet I was quite unable to free myself from the grip of this horrible feeling that paralyzed my whole being. Frank went on:

"You asked me to be frank with you, Mr. Heimler. So I'm being frank. I don't believe that a Jew would want to help a 'goy' unless he was getting something out of it. Since the day that you crucified our Lord, you have been bleeding decent Christians for centuries. That is why you have had to pay such a high price in recent years."

Memories flooded through me. I am six years old on the way to school. In front of a church is a crucifix with the bleeding suffering Man, His eyes turning towards heaven.... "You see that?" A big boy of fourteen stands in my way. "You see that, you bastard of a Jew? You did that to Him." "It's a lie," I scream. "It's a lie." My nose is bleeding, where he struck me in the face, and the blood soaks my shirt. I run, run. "You were beaten, Jancsi," says my headmaster, Mr. Bonyhadi, "because you are a Jew. But you must not believe that all Christians are wicked. No, you must not believe that, my son." And he washes my face.

It is the spring of 1941 in Hungary. Soldiers, *our* Hungarian soldiers in uniform, fifteen of them, are waiting around the corner till an old Jew appears. The fifteen men throw themselves on him ... I am a silent, impotent witness. "Help, help," I shout – but the passersby do not seem to hear. The sergeant orders his men into line: it is all over. The old man looks like a ragged doll with red paint poured over him. I try to help him as he prays: "Hear, oh Israel, our Lord our God, Our Lord is one ... Blessed be His name for ever and ever." He would never walk again.

"Father, what have we done to deserve all this?" My father stands by the window and looks towards the distant hills of Koszeg.

"What have we done? I will tell you, son. We have given the world the Ten Commandments, the Prophets, and Jesus too. We have given the world law and order; we have shown mankind the path to a good life. But these things are not easily forgiven us. Each time a Jew is beaten, the law we gave the world is beaten. Be proud to belong to a people who are beaten in the name of justice."

The pictures rise and fade ... terrible pictures now, of Auschwitz, Dr. Mengele ... right, left, right, left ... Where is God? There is nothing but blood. Where is God?

"God?" said the old Rabbi. "Of course He is there, in pain, and beyond pain, eternal. Whether you die, or I did, He is there just the same. Pray, my son. You are not alone ... thousands are with you. Pray, as your ancestors did when tortured by the Popes, and Kings and Princes of an insane world."

The present slowly returned – the pub ... the people ... Frank. Now what shall I do? Shall I walk off, with the curse of two thousand years? No, I can't. Frank Latham hates me, not because I am myself, but because of his own unhappiness. Oh God, give me strength to see that. Give me strength to help him, despite myself. What did the Prophet Isaiah say? "Be light unto the gentiles!" Oh God, help me to be a small, flickering light, to him, to myself. Let me, the persecuted, cure the persecutor of his hate. Are we not both the victim of it?

At last I said to Frank:

"You are trying to hurt me, because you cannot yet believe in my good intentions. You want to put me to the test to find out whether I shall let you down. But I shall not let you down. We have got to see this thing through together."

His eyes were shining, but not with hate. They were the eyes of a child – lost, frightened and guilty. He was weeping.

"Forgive me Mr. H. I didn't know what I was saying. I didn't really mean to hurt you."

A feeling of great peace came over me, such as I had seldom known before. We had both found, through this ordeal, a new meaning to our lives.

* * *

Several of my colleagues were not much impressed by my methods. Some politely, others somewhat impatiently, expressed the view that my involvement with the patient and my discarding of more formal methods were signs of charlatanism, and might also be dangerous. There must be a line of demarcation, they considered, between personal and professional relationships. These colleagues were mostly working in mental hospitals or child guidance clinics, under the direction of or in close partnership with a psychiatrist. I in turn accused them of imitating doctors and imputed many reasons for this. I suggested that because they wished to be psychotherapists themselves and could not, they were now offering psychotherapy and water. I also suggested that they were dependent on the psychiatrist because they needed a "father" to tell them what to do and what not to do. I hinted that I felt it was a sign of immaturity to tolerate the domination of the psychiatrist. They then turned the tables on me by asking if my own attitude to psychiatrists was not suggestive of infantile rebellion, presumably arising from my relationship with my own father. We had some stormy meetings, and for some time, convinced that I was right and they were wrong, I was not too popular in my profession. I dismissed their criticism of emotional involvement by telling myself that my English colleagues had a defective capacity for feeling. I fancied myself a heretic, and I played the role of the misunderstood pioneer.

Then, towards the end of 1955, I met Betty Irvine, a very experienced teacher of our profession, who was holding an evening course on the application of analytical theories in casework. The discussions were interesting, and to my amazement Betty did not seem shocked by my "unusual" methods nor consider me to be a heretic or a charlatan. She frequently said, in fact, that there is room for any member of differing techniques in psychiatric casework, as long as they *work*, and as long as one tries to understand why they work, with what kind of patient and in what situation. To my surprise the other members of the group seemed to agree. Moreover, they pressed me to evaluate and conceptualize my own methods. Feeling no longer misunderstood I began to ask myself questions that I had only half asked hitherto, and I also began to find better answers.

When the course was finished, I found that I wanted to continue our discussions and to put further questions to her. I began to drop in to her Hampstead flat for an occasional chat.

We were sitting there one evening by the fire, drinking our coffee and discussing professional problems deep into the night. Beyond the window was a clear winter sky, and the naked branches of the tall trees were silhouetted against a frozen moon.

"You say people don't understand you," she said thoughtfully, "but how can they understand you, if you don't explain *why* you do the things you do?"

"But I did explain why."

She had a habit of thinking for a few seconds after one had finished a sentence. Then she would nod as if in agreement, but in fact this only indicated that she understood what one meant. Sometimes this was disconcerting. She nodded now.

"No, John," she answered at last (my English friends, like Robert in Budapest, were unable to pronounce the Hungarian *Jancsi*), "you don't really explain *why* you do whatever you do. You don't go much beyond telling us *what* you do."

"Well," I replied, "take Frank, for example. I told you all the details of the case. Do you or don't you agree that I was right to go for a walk with him?"

Once more she nodded, waited for a few minutes, swallowed, and said:

"Why do you think it was necessary?"

I was slightly annoyed. I had told her already that Frank hated the atmosphere of my office; that he could not fit into an established framework. Why should I have to repeat all that now?

"I think," she said, "that there is a little more to it than that. Isn't it that you felt he wanted to test out your feelings, your friendship? Didn't you feel that he wanted to see if you really were different from that psychiatrist who wouldn't look at him? You didn't really go out with Frank in the first instance just because it would be easier for him, but because you wanted to prove to him that you could be trusted."

"Yes."

"Well, then," she went on after a few seconds, "you chose not to interpret why he wanted you to go out with him, as some of your colleagues would do, but you decided to do as he asked. In other words, you were doing a little psychodrama, because Frank's extreme mistrust of people made him unable to believe what they said. Frank seems to be one of those people for whom deeds speak louder than words. No doubt you felt, as you said, that it would be impossible to find words which would allay Frank's misgivings, and the only way to relieve them would be to prove something by your actions."

She was, of course, right. It was not that she was telling me anything new about my motives; rather, she was helping me to put them into words. This ability to verbalize my half-digested thoughts and feelings was Betty's main contribution to me at that time. She went on:

"And what did you talk about in the park?"

I told her about my conversation with Frank.

"Well, it seems to me that this was still a professional interview, even if the setting was not a conventional one. It wasn't at all an ordinary social occasion, was it?"

"But I wasn't interpreting in the ordinary way."

"Wasn't it a sort of interpretation when you remarked on his choice of seat? No, I see what you mean, you were commenting on his behavior which was symbolic of his whole way of life, and he recognized it as such, and that seemed to set him off explaining his motivation himself.... But it isn't so different really from the usual technique, is it? You are still aiming at helping him to achieve insight, by a slightly different method."

"Yes, but I think it is important that I am interpreting *behavior*. I go with him into a social situation and then I can see his problems in action, and draw his attention to them."

"Yes, and then you made another kind of interpretation, when you related this behavior to his early experience, just as you would in the office. So the difference really is that instead of interpreting what he *tells* you about his social contacts, about some episode which is already past, you interpret his social behavior *as it occurs* in the situation.... This brought him a lot closer to you, didn't it? You might never have heard those confidences in the office ... and probably you would never have been exposed to that anti-Semitic outburst either. He would not have felt safe enough with you, and you would not have mattered so much to him; he would not have needed to put you to such a drastic test."

"I will tell you another thing," I said, lighting a cigarette, "I wouldn't have *felt* it so much if it had happened in the office. There was a ghastly moment in the pub when I was full of all those memories he had stirred up, and the pain of them, when I very much regretted having left the safety of my office. Before I went out with him the first time I felt this too, that the whole setting of the office, the desk, my chair, the patient's chair, the familiar yet impersonal atmosphere, is all a necessary buffer against too much involvement. But I still think there are some patients one cannot help unless one leaves that shelter – though one certainly has to work much harder not to take it personally and to remember that it is all part of the problem. That's what makes it different from an ordinary social situation."

"But you can see why it might not be reasonable to expect everyone else to work in this way? Not many people survived Auschwitz, after all. I think there are plenty of patients, who can be helped in the traditional ways, don't you? On the other hand, you are not the only one who is experimenting with untraditional methods. I saw an article just the other day by two people who were working and thinking on similar lines. And I don't think it is reasonable to expect the rest of us to expose ourselves to the kind of strain you felt in the pub, without the support of an experienced psychiatric consultant – who might have been able, incidentally, to help you with your own emotions ... but this is just by the way. I think you have got something there, but you can't expect other people to use this method too, or teachers to teach it, until you have described it much more clearly and explained the differences, and why you feel your technique is more useful for certain patients. Perhaps you ought to write an article about this."

* * *

Driving home that night I thought of many things. Betty's attempt to clarify my ideas had removed a barrier and through the opening now flooded a torrent of thoughts about my work. As I was driving over Hampstead Heath, I remembered the episode of the key on that very heath many years ago. How different my problems seemed now. I thought of my many patients, and of the painful fact that there were so many things I still did not understand. Why, for example, do wives sometimes break down when their husbands recover? Why do fathers often face emotional crises when their children are successfully treated? What secret bond connects members of families to each other? Is it possible that by treating an individual one may do harm to others who are not treated, or should one treat the whole family, and if so, how?

The heater of my car was not working, and it was very cold. Mist condensed on the window, and I had to stop to wipe it off. It reminded me how little I really know, how much of my professional life was still obscured by mist. Would I become wiser as the years went by?

"The child is father to the man." This was one of the statements I had discussed in my examination papers when I qualified as a psychiatric social worker. Now in the middle of the night at Hendon Central I asked aloud: "If the child is father to the man, who is mother to Man?" A policeman passing on a motorbike looked at me oddly, and I blushed, imagining he might think I had gone crazy, talking to myself like that. What shapes Man apart from his childhood experiences? Where, indeed, is the "mother"?

I used to visit an old lady at Crouch End, who lived in one of those large Victorian houses by herself. Her lace curtains, faded carpets and furniture were all witnesses of a bygone age. Her husband had died a few years before, and her money was running short. One day she realized that if she wanted to keep her house, she would have to let some rooms. She started with the basement. It was nicely decorated, and eventually a family moved in. The man worked in a factory, and the wife had a part-time job in an office canteen; the two children, both in their twenties, were also in jobs. They were a happy family, and they had enough money to have a good time. While watching television on Saturday night there was plenty of beer for everyone, and their laughter was loud and happy. But these alien noises not only changed the atmosphere of the old house, they hurt the old lady. Alone and unhappy, as time went on she developed the idea that these strangers were purposely trying to annoy her with their carefree ways. When she wanted to listen to Mozart and Beethoven, the voice of Tommy Steel intruded from below. By the time the upper part of the house was let, she felt a refugee in her own house. The people upstairs had teenage sons, whose main preoccupation was quarrelling about the motorcycle parked in front of the house. The old lady could hear every word from both above and below, and at times she thought she would go out of her mind. And she did.

She complained to her doctor that all these people were against her, that they wanted her to die so that they could take over the whole house. She, who had been so gentle and quiet all her life, now became intolerant and rude. When the motorbike was revved up at night, she would scream out of the window: "Stop that noise." When the radio or television was on, she would bang on the floor or ceiling. This "paranoia" of hers was not the result only of her childhood problems, but also that of a changing age that kept her short of money and forced these strangers into her house. That the cause of an emotional breakdown or mental illness might lie in the pressures of society gave me a clue, as I arrived home, as to who the "mother" might be. If the child was father to the Man, then Society was undoubtedly the mother.

* * *

One afternoon, a friend of mine and I were sitting in an espresso bar in Golders Green, talking about our past. There were a number of people sitting around us, most of them foreigners – for Golders Green was, and still is, a foreign island in the British sea. My friend asked me whether in England the police would spy on people to discover their political beliefs. I said that this was unlikely, because in England the police only "spied" on criminals. We were talking quite loud, and I looked around, a little afraid that we might have caused some interest to the other patrons of the coffee bar, but no one even turned a head. I said to my friend: "I bet that if we had this conversation six miles away from here, we would be the center of interest."

Then I said to him: "Say again, as loud as you can, that you are afraid that the police may be after you." He did so, and a woman in her fifties turned round, just for a fleeting second, but no one else took any notice. We concluded from this that most of these people must have experienced persecution in their past, in Germany under the Nazis or in Eastern Europe under the Communists. To prove our point we drove on to Southgate, and had a cup of tea in a teashop, surrounded by middle-class ladies and one or two middle-aged gentlemen. My friend said again: "At times I cannot help feeling that the police are after me." This time every head turned in our direction, and they all looked at us in icy silence, as if we were criminals of the worst kind. Not one of them knew from experience that innocent people can be persecuted by the police. Here, if the police were after people, there was always a good reason for it.

After this episode, the thought came to me that an area like that of Golders Green might perhaps more easily accept someone with a persecution mania. I wondered if a Continental employer, for example, would find a man with such paranoid ideas easier to tolerate than would a British employer who had never had to face the experience of persecution. Was it possible, in fact, that someone who had experienced real persecution would be less frightened of a mentally ill patient with delusions of persecution? I was able to put my theory to the test with some success when I placed a man with such a delusion (of seventeen years' standing) in employment of this kind, at which he is still working. Six miles away, in Southgate, this man would have represented a threat to a British employer and the test could not have been carried out.

CHAPTER THREE

During the following year, Frank Latham was working as a traveler. The old vicious circle was now broken, and for the first time for many years he was able to provide for his wife and child. At first Evelyn, his wife, was relieved and happy at the change, but gradually she became depressed and restless, and for reasons she could not understand had fits of crying. Frank, who had kept in touch with me quite regularly during that year, now asked me to see her. He felt that at this stage his wife needed my help perhaps more than he did.

Accordingly, I went to see Evelyn, whom I had only met once or twice before, about a year ago, at the time when Frank started working. I had more than one reason to see her this time, for because of her depression and her inability to go on loving her husband, Frank now felt that he did not need her any more. He had met another woman.

Evelyn was born illegitimately and knew nothing about her parents. She had been brought up by a man and woman whom she called uncle and aunt, but they had never told her how she came to them. There was some unspoken mystery about her origin, as though it had been a dreadful disease, and she learned not to inquire as the years went by. Uncle and aunt had been good to her and she spoke with real affection of them, and yet she had always felt that something was missing. She had been searching for it throughout her life, without knowing what it was she was looking for.

"It is like being pregnant, you know," she told me, "and wanting a particular food without knowing what food. When we first got married, I thought I had found it at last, but even that was not what I was looking for. When the baby came I hoped again that I had found it, and yet after a few weeks I realized that I had not. When Frank was ill and needed me as a child needs his mother, I thought I had found it in helping him, but now he doesn't need me anymore, and I feel incomplete. It is awful to say that although I am grateful to you, there are times when I curse your name because you have taken something away from me."

I asked her what I had taken from her, and when she did not answer I asked her whether she was perhaps disappointed with me because now Frank needed her less. She replied that this was true, but that the very admission of it filled her with horror and a sense of guilt.

"Sometimes I feel," she went on, "as if I want to run. Run out into the snow and the rain and the cold to find a place where I can find what I have lost. I fancy somehow that there must be such a place. I used to go to church, but I could not find it there. Death is the nearest to it, I think. I somehow think that death must be a lovely place. Like a dreamless sleep. The end of everything."

We had many talks like this without any noticeable result. But by now I had learned that the spoken word does not always relieve the heart. I had to wait for the spring to come in more than one sense.

It was at this time that Frank came to me and said that he had fallen in love with someone else. He told me that he felt that Evelyn wanted him to be sick and dependent; that she was ill herself because he was well. But now he did not want to be mothered anymore; he wanted to feel that he was a man. And so the inevitable had happened; he had met a married woman, unhappy with her husband, in whom, he believed, he had found what he wanted in life; someone with sex appeal, a real woman who needed him as a man. It was this relationship that gave me the clue. Frank had now left the emotional baby stage, but he had not yet grown beyond the years of childhood. Evelyn had been the good mother who put up with him. He had needed her to act out the past, but without the catastrophic result of being sent away from home. But that stage had passed, and Evelyn had outlived the purpose for which he had created her. Was it possible, I asked myself, that this new affair might be the turning point in the relationship between husband and wife? Could Evelyn now grow into a woman who would want her mate? Frank had told her about his affair, and now she had to face the fact that either she must desire her husband as a man or else their marriage was finished for good.

And it was in competition with the unknown woman that Evelyn at last found what she was looking for. Now she allowed herself to be what she had always wanted to be, someone who dared to demand her rights for her own sake. She changed during these weeks, in a dramatic and beautiful way. As the spring brings forth its flowers, as the earth is blessed by the mysterious sap of life, Evelyn started to vibrate with new life. She opened her heart and her body at last to a love that she had not known before.

For both Frank and Evelyn it was the beginning of a new road, along which they could walk together because they had found the love they had sought for so long.

I could now slowly fade out of their lives and enter the lives of others.

*   *   *

During these years, I not only gained more confidence in myself, but the satisfaction of my work permeated the whole of my life. I had found at last the peace and security I so much needed. I felt that my roots were going deeper, that I belonged here, in England, at last.

MY LIFE AFTER AUSCHWITZ

Then, at the end of October, from some hundreds of miles away in the shadow of the Carpathian Mountains, came the news of the Hungarian revolution. Overnight the peace of my mind was shattered. I was back again in spirit on that bloodstained earth that had seen so many revolutions against oppressors in the past. It was almost as if part of me was fighting in the streets of Budapest. And when the Russian tanks and guns managed at last to suppress the four days' freedom, I was precipitated into grief for the fate of my native land. But my grief was not only for the result of the unsuccessful revolution: I heard news that during that brief period those elements that had tried to destroy us during the war were becoming active once more. Whilst the majority of Hungarians sincerely wanted freedom and a new way of life, a minority of Nazis had emerged from their rat holes to finish what they had started during the war.

I now decided to write a book about my own past experiences, on behalf of those tortured and exterminated millions who could no longer speak for themselves; and so my first book, *Night of the Mist*, slowly took shape. The bitterness and pain of my still open wounds flowed into the pages, and I worked night after night, sometimes into the early hours of the morning. Strangely, I was never tired, and after a few hours' sleep I could start my day afresh. Lily by my side was the dividing line between the past and the present, and it was her presence that made it possible for me to close my eyes in untroubled sleep.

At last, on October 24, 1957, almost a year after the Hungarian Revolution, I stood in front of the Commissioner for Oaths in Hendon, and swore the Oath of Allegiance, holding the Old Testament in my hand:

> I, Jeno Heimler, known as Eugene Heimler, swear by Almighty God that I will be faithful and bear true Allegiance to Her Majesty Queen

MY LIFE AFTER AUSCHWITZ

Elizabeth the Second, Her Heirs and Successors, according to Law.

For the first time in my life I had equal rights as a citizen.

These were years of feverish activity, in which my work, my book, and also my attempt to help in establishing Jewish communal life occupied me fully. My chance to do the last came when a small Jewish community in the new town of Harlow in Essex needed some help.

I was not entirely unprepared for this important task. I came from a religious background, and since the age of four I had attended Hebrew classes, and later in my teens I went to the local Talmud Torah school where I studied our ancient literature. I could read Hebrew as well as Hungarian and some years ago I could translate the Bible from the original into my native tongue. Now I used once more what I had been taught as a young man. On Friday nights I would drive down to hold the Sabbath services and sing the songs of my people; songs which had survived the bodies of my tortured ancestors, who, unlike me, had never been allowed a safe corner in a so-called Christian world. The same words and melodies that were sung in the ghettoes of past centuries now once more sounded in a modern English town in the middle of the twentieth century, proclaiming our unbroken faith and our belief in a better life. I sensed then that our survival is no coincidence. Man may destroy man's body, but no man can destroy man's spirit. My small contribution in Harlow was to me a great victory over my former adversaries, over those who believed that they could annihilate us.

Today, as I write these words, I realize why I did all that I did in those years. Not only through faith, but because of fear and guilt, I was trying to rebuild what had been destroyed, and in doing so I was slowly healing my own wounds. It was as if by expressing as much as I could, I was breathing new life into myself and into those who needed my life.

MY LIFE AFTER AUSCHWITZ

* * *

When Britain opened her doors to thousands of refugees after the Hungarian Revolution, I offered my services for one afternoon a week to various refugee organizations in assisting them with some of the problems that were bound to come up in connection with those who sought a new way of life. I did this because I knew that there were not many Hungarian speaking qualified social workers, and because I realized that the handling and understanding of refugees was a complex matter. Some of those former compatriots of mine were disturbed people who could not settle down in their new environment; some were mentally ill and needed treatment; and a great many were bewildered by a strange culture and at a complete loss to know how and where to start. In many instances families had been broken up, and individuals were finding it hard to carry on life without their beloved ones. Some adventurers arrived, too, who believed that the Thames ran with gold; others were Fascists or Communists who thought that here anything was allowed, confusing freedom with license. As I spoke their native tongue all these people confided in me, and I tried to help them by word and deed, by explanation of this new culture, and by interpreting their needs to my fellow Britons. I found these afternoons absorbing, until one day in the winter of 1956 I came face to face with a young man in his early twenties who wanted to commit suicide. I have met others who had suicidal thoughts, but what was so strange about this young man was the way in which he questioned the sanity of those who wanted to live. He was rather small, thin and pale, wearing an outworn raincoat as he sat shivering in front of me. He lived near Paddington Station in a furnished room. The room was small and cold, and from one day to another he did not see a soul to speak to. Not only did he feel isolated from others in this strange new world by the fact that neighbors and strangers had their own problems and were not too friendly, but also because he could speak no English.

"I feel," he said, "as I did during the war, when mother and I were hiding from the Nazis."

I asked him whether the reason he had been in hiding was because he was Jewish.

He shook his head.

"No, I am not Jewish. Mother was born a Jewess but my father was a Catholic. He was an officer in the Hungarian Army, and he was killed during the war. We were living in our flat in the Jozef Boulevard, and everything would have been all right, but mother looked so Jewish. I shall never forget...." He went on, gazing into nothingness. "I saw it from the window. I saw the bastard with the swastika on his arm raising his gun. I saw mother producing her identity card, and then I saw her fall and the bastard standing over her body laughing. I must have been about ten at the time."

"What happened to you then?"

"I was looked after by some friends and then, when the war ended, I became an apprentice engineer."

"Are you interested in engineering?"

"Not much."

"Why did you pick on engineering, then?"

"I didn't pick on it. My guardian did. He was an engineer."

"And what happened then, after you completed your apprenticeship?"

"I worked."

"Had you many friends?"

"A few."

"Girlfriends too?"

Gyuszi turned away, and for the first time since he had started talking to me, I saw an emotional reaction. He wept quietly, and I did not disturb him. I was relieved that he could show his feelings, but I was also alarmed because I did not know much about this young man. Minutes went by. At last he spoke again.

"I met Gizi in 1953. August, it was. She was a university student and came out to our factory with a group of other students. There was a Party talk, and she led a discussion group afterwards. I remember I asked her some questions. I asked her who manipulated the Party machine; who framed the Party's policy; how the Party could act on behalf of the working class when people were only told about the decisions? I remember Gizi giving me some answers, but I don't remember what she actually said – only that she was pretty and I very much wanted to take her out. It took me days afterwards to find her address, and then we met. She was the first woman I ever loved."

Gyuszi stopped again, as if undecided whether to go on or not.

"We met regularly," he continued at last, "at least once a week, and we spoke freely to each other about our doubts, about Rakoczi, about Stalin and Russian Imperialism. We talked about poetry and love too. One night, quite late, I went home to my lodging after being with Gizi. I opened my door and moved my hand to switch on the light, when somebody spoke from the darkened room: 'If I were you, comrade, I would not put that light on.' I couldn't make it out. At first I thought it was a burglar, but what would a burglar be doing in *my* place. It also crossed my mind, that if it was a burglar he must have a strange sense of humor to call me 'comrade.'

"The light from an electric torch shone into my eyes, and the voice addressed me once more:

"'Perhaps you would be kind enough to sit down.' I sat down, and asked: 'Who the hell do you think you are? What sort of stupid joke is this?' Now another voice laughed in the dark and said to the first one: 'Did you hear that, he really wants to know who we are?' They laughed again. I realized then, that this was no joke.

"'We are going to have a little chat,' said the owner of the first voice. 'A little chat, that's all.' Then he said seriously: 'We are members of the Political Police, and we want to ask you a few questions.'"

Gyuszi once more interrupted his narrative, looking blankly ahead. He sat for some time without moving, and then went on with his story, speaking more freely now.

"I asked the policemen what I could do for them, and was told to shut up, that questions were only asked by the police. I was ordered to get up, to go to the door, and as if nothing had happened, to walk across the corridor, down the staircase and into the waiting car. I was told that if I made one false move I would get it in the back. I did what they told me, of course. Throughout the fifteen minutes' journey neither of the detectives talked to me, and when I asked them where they were taking to me and why, I received no answer. I was in a cold sweat of fear now. I kept on asking myself what I had done, but however hard I tried, I could not find the answer.

"We arrived at a building and the two men accompanied me, again without a word, down a long corridor to a cell. They pushed me into this in darkness, and I could hear the door being locked from the outside.

"I tried to find my way in the dark to a bed or a chair, but there seemed to be none, so I sat on the floor. I found a cigarette and some matches in my jacket, and lit a cigarette: I was thankful that so far these had not been taken from me. Then I tried to concentrate. What had I done? What could the charge be? I tried to work out what time it was, and concluded that it must be about half past one at night. I lit a match, and noticed some writing on the wall, Christian names of men and women. One screamed into the darkness: 'Oh God, help me!' The match burned down. They were too precious to use any more, so I sat in the darkness, waiting.

"Waiting for what? Why didn't they come? The silence became quite unbearable, and I got up and started to beat my fists against the iron door. I shouted, I cursed and I cried, but no one answered.

"I spent a miserable night, but when morning came, I still did not see any light. The cell was pitch dark, yet some air came in from somewhere. I felt hungry, tired and quite exhausted. Filthy, too. I longed for a bath more than anything.

"Later in the day, when I had completely lost all sense of time, a uniformed guard opened the door and handed me some bread and coffee. He asked me with perfect politeness if I had any complaint; there was not the slightest irony in his voice. I in turn asked the guard why I was being held and what was going to happen, to which he replied that he was only a guard and not an investigator.

"It was not till dawn on the second day that I was sent for. I walked between two guards to a well-lit office on the third floor, where a tall thin man wearing thick spectacles sat behind a large desk. When I entered, he raised himself in his chair and offered me a cigarette.

"'Won't you sit down, please?'

"The guards left the room. By the window sat a shorthand typist, ready to take notes.

"'Well, now,' said the man, 'why do you think you are here?'

"'I haven't got a clue. Perhaps you will tell me.'

"The man wearing thick spectacles turned towards the stenographer.

"'Will you please put down, that when questioned, the accused stated that he did not know the reason for his arrest.'

"Then, turning to me, he said: 'So you are determined to be difficult from the start?'

"'I don't know what I am supposed to have done, so what else can I say?'

"The man did not let that pass.

"'You know quite well what the charge against you is, so you had better confess. It won't help you if you don't, I assure you.'

"I burst out in despair:

"'But I don't know! For God's sake, let us stop playing the fool.'

"'As far as God is concerned,' said the man 'we had better leave Him out of this. And as for playing the fool, you will soon find out that we are not in the mood for play.' He stopped for a few seconds and looked through some papers before going on:

"'Look, Mr. Vandor, there is no point in going on with this interview. You have obviously decided to deny the charge against you, by pretending that you don't know what it is. I shall give you another few days to think it over…'

"At this point I lost my temper.

"'Now, look here,' I shouted, 'what have you got against me? I have not done anything against the law, as far as I know. I have not killed anyone, I have not been stealing, nor have I blackmailed any living soul, I am certainly not a spy. I am not against this régime; I couldn't possibly be that, considering that the Nazis killed my mother when I was a child. As a citizen of this country, I demand as my right to know with what I am charged. Failing that, I want the services of a lawyer. What you are doing is criminal, it's inhuman.'

"'Are you suggesting,' said the man with the spectacles, 'that our legal and social system is also inhuman? Now we are getting a little bit nearer to the truth.'

"'You turn everything inside out, and upside down. You want me to give myself away…'

MY LIFE AFTER AUSCHWITZ

"The man pushed a bell, and when the two guards appeared at the door, they took me back to my dark cell."

When Gyuszi reached this point in his story, he stared at me for some minutes, as if I was the interrogator on that fateful night. Then he repeated again and again: "I tell you there is no point in living; I cannot understand why anyone wants to go on living."

"What happened to you after that night?" I asked, as if I had not heard his remark.

Again he sat looking at me with an expression of bewilderment. I said, smiling: "I am not that police officer, you know." A very faint smile passed over his face.

"For a few days nothing happened. I was given food and drink; I was taken for my daily walk in a small courtyard. No one talked to me. I wondered if there were other prisoners in that place, but I never saw a soul except the guards. As the days passed I came to the conclusion that I must give them some confession, something, anything, because if things went on for long like this, I should go crazy. So I became my own attorney, and started to accuse myself of things I had thought and done.

"I don't know if you will understand what I am going to tell you now." He looked at me, and I saw fear in his eyes. "Perhaps you can't understand, but I'll tell you, all the same. I began to wonder whether everything that was happening was either a nightmare or the hell of which I had learnt when I was a child. Was it possible that I was answering now for my sins against the moral law, for those times during my adolescent years when I had secretly sought the pleasure of my own body in disgust and guilt? Was it possible that I was being punished because I did not go to confession ... that I was paying the price for making love to Gizi? And when Gizi came into my mind, an irresistible desire swept over me, holding my muscles rigid and my veins tight ... till I felt as though I was an adolescent again, ready to sin once more. Then I imagined that the man in the spectacles was watching me in the darkness of my cell, that he could see everything I was doing ... and I felt like a hunted animal. I stood in the corner of my cell, and ... and I soiled myself....

"Then I realized that the man in the spectacles was right: I was wicked; I had sinned, a mortal sin. I banged on the door. I wanted to see him, to confess ... but no one came.

"When I had calmed down a little I remembered something else: how I had questioned Gizi that first day during the public meeting on how policy was formulated by the Party. Yes, that was it. Someone must have reported me, and they must have read rebellion into those questions ... and they were right ... there was rebellion ... against the rulers ... I must tell him that.

"They came for me again at what I imagined was dawn.

"'Well, Mr. Vandor?' said the man. 'Have you now clarified your mind?'

"'Yes, I have.'

"'Oh, good, very good. Will you have a cigarette?'

"I wanted to speak, to confess, to say everything that was in my heart, but the man did not let me speak.

"'Instead of talking about these things, perhaps it would be better if you wrote them down. Please sit down at the stenographer's desk; we shan't need her today, anyway. Here is pencil and paper, and pen and ink. I shall not trouble you at all; I shall just sit here and go on with my work.'

"He left me a few cigarettes, and I sat down to write.

"I wrote something like this:

> I, the undersigned Gyula Vandor, hereby state that I make this confession of my own free will, without being forced or influenced in any way.

At a meeting some time ago, I wanted to know how the Party policy was being formulated, how it could be done without previous consultation with the working classes on whose behalf the Party was supposed to act. I realize now that behind this question there was skepticism in regard to the wisdom of our leaders. I am very sorry for my weakness, but I will try to correct it in the future. Signed Gyula Vandor.

"The spectacled one read it, and without a word showed me to the door, where the guards were waiting to take me back to my cell. I felt happier now. They could not punish me very severely because of that, I thought.

"An hour later they came for me again, waking me from a heavy sleep.

"The man in spectacles was looking worried.

"'Mr. Vandor, there are a few questions that I would like to ask you before we both retire for the night. First, did you know a woman called Gizella Szilvagyi?'

"My heart beat fast at the mention of Gizi's name.

"'Yes, indeed I know her.'

"'Do you mind if I ask what was the relationship between you two?'

"'I do mind,' I answered. 'What has this got to do with my case?'

"'You must leave my reason to me,' said the spectacled one. 'Now, let's have it straight. Were you lovers?'

"I did not answer.

"'I repeat my question again: were you lovers?'

"'Yes.'

"'Thank you.'

"What followed then was like a nightmare. The man in spectacles opened up file after file, informing me that Gizi had been involved in a conspiracy against the Republic, and because I had been her lover I must have known about it, and thus be a conspirator also. I was told that I had two ways open to me: either to admit it, in which case the Court would take my confession into consideration; or to deny it, in which case Gizi's own testimony was enough to get me a very severe sentence, perhaps death itself. I was told that the fact of my being only nineteen would not be taken into account, because many young men could be more dangerous than old ones. I denied the charge. I was not tortured in any way, but I was deported to an internment camp without ever being brought to trial. I stayed in the camp until the Revolution, when I came to England. I do not know why I came, but I know now that there is no solution for me either here or anywhere else. There is no purpose in life any more.... The only solution is in death."

"And what happened to Gizi?" I asked.

He shook his head. He did not know.

One of the most difficult aspects of my professional life is having to face my inability to assist someone who turns to me for help. For the many I have assisted, there are about an equal number of people whom I have been unable to help. Gyuszi Vandor was one of them. He walked out of my office that afternoon never to return. His problems were real enough, but although I knew that he had very little wish to live, I also knew that he was not insane and therefore could not be made to go to hospital. He disappeared from England, and I never knew what became of him. He was broken by a crazy society, by the insane world of which we are all a part.

MY LIFE AFTER AUSCHWITZ

CHAPTER FOUR

My attempt to help the "work-shy" resulted in an experiment which today goes under the name of the "Hendon Experiment."

Frank was right when he assumed that there was some understanding between myself and the National Assistance Board; but he put the wrong interpretation on my connection with the Board. He accused me, during that unforgettable interview in the pub, of working hand in hand with the National Assistance Board as I could not bear to see money going to a man like him. Nothing was farther from the truth. I was not concerned with the financial side when the Hendon Experiment began; only with the unhappiness that unemployment is bound to bring about. I saw in those terrible camps in Germany what meaningless tasks could do to people's minds. I remember how a group of people broke down in the camp of Troeglitz when the SS ordered them to move some sand from one place to another and then to move it back. Some were driven insane; others became so objectionable, even by concentration camp standards, that trouble was inevitable; and one or two committed suicide. I also saw in the same camp, and later in Buchenwald, the other side of the coin. I saw how people were able to maintain their sanity by doing some job of work that had a purpose and a meaning. When I had approached the National Assistance Board in the first instance, this vague memory was at the back of my mind. I honestly believe that those people who for any reason cannot work must eventually destroy themselves, either morally or physically, or destroy the people around them. Work, I found, is closely connected with the human instincts, and if an instinct is blocked, it can destroy the individual.

Ron Bradfield, the Area Officer of the National Assistance Board in Hendon, understood only too well what I meant. With great insight he saw, too, that applicants to the Board only present one aspect of themselves, and that it was desirable to learn more about the hidden facets of their personality. He agreed with me that our mutual cooperation could bring forth nothing but good, and introduced me to his colleagues on the Board, with whom I discussed ways in which the applicants could be helped. They taught me a great deal. I learned what goes on during the interview between the applicant and the Board Officer; the kind of difficulties that the officers have to face; the kind of limitations that are set by their official role and shortage of time. I told them about psychiatric social work, expressing the hope that our cooperation might result not only in money saved for the State, but in something which is not measurable – human happiness.

As time went on, I found that my prejudices against civil servants were undergoing considerable change. Before the Hendon Experiment I had viewed civil servants, British or otherwise, with great suspicion. I had considered most of them as mere computing machines, completely forgetting that behind the mask of the civil servant was a human being like myself. How refreshing it was now to meet these people, some truly dedicated to their work! They smiled at my prejudices when I felt brave enough to tell them, and proceeded to tell me about their own prejudices against representatives of the psychiatric profession. With some cynicism they talked about "trick-cyclists," about the unpopular army questionnaires and psychological tests, black magic, mesmerism. They resented that it is such people who are supposed to be experts in human relations, questioning whether anyone can learn from books about human beings. They said that psychiatric practitioners talk a language no one can understand; that they cannot even understand it themselves. It is true enough that some social workers and psychiatrists use psychiatric jargon as a form of self-defense; in fact, the impression some doctors and social workers convey is that they live in an ivory tower and do not speak the common language of mankind. But it is because psychiatry is so insecure that they have to imitate other specialists, and it was this insecurity that was translated as nonsensical by the Board's officers. Moreover, psychological concepts are not easy to digest. The dynamic aspect of the mind appears to many people as a threatening one, and civil servants are no exception. Ridicule and laughter, antagonism and sarcasm, are all expressions of a rejection of the truth. For the first time in my professional life I could see the point of view of both camps, and this indeed was an eye-opener.

By the end of 1957, we could draw some conclusions about the Hendon Experiment. By that time I had written a few articles in which some of the results were evaluated, and the figures showed without a shadow of doubt that the cooperation between the Board and myself was being successful in assisting people to regain their position in society. During the year of the experiment, the National Assistance Board had referred forty-one persons to me, and it was estimated that the saving to National Assistance had been somewhere around £1,600. All the people concerned were long-term unemployment cases, and if this figure had been multiplied by four hundred, i.e. if the experiment could have been carried out by the four hundred offices of the National Assistance Board, each office referring forty cases to a psychiatric social worker, in one year the national saving could have been £600,000. A single person, unemployed and in need of National Assistance, was at that time receiving fifty shillings per week.

I mentioned in my articles that it might be worthwhile for the National Assistance Board to look into this matter very carefully; for it might well be that in the future the adjustment to work of people drawing National Assistance could be undertaken by the Board's officers themselves. This might be brought about gradually by consultation on individual cases between psychiatric social workers and the Board's officers, which would in time lead to the latter being able to handle the emotional as well as the material problems of the people who came to them. I also felt by the end of 1957 that although the welfare state provided so many forms of assistance besides financial help for those who were in need of it, these should not necessarily be considered the final answer to our social problems. The situation, in fact, was similar to that of a home where the material needs were provided for the child, but where for various reasons his emotional needs were not fully met. It was my opinion that the welfare state should extend its facilities beyond the many existing services, and should make provision for the emotional needs of the people who find it necessary to apply for National Assistance.

Ron Bradfield and I talked a great deal about this during these years. But I remember specifically one talk we had under a Christmas tree in his Hampstead flat, in the winter of 1957. Our respective wives in the other room were occupied with our noisy children, and we two sat and discussed the past and the future.

"Tell me this," said Ron. "How could the Hendon Experiment be extended to other parts of the country?"

"The only way, I think, would be to find some of my colleagues who would be interested in working as closely as I have with the Board."

"But most of your colleagues are not interested in working with us," he said. "They are already committed to work in hospitals and clinics."

"Only because Community Care is rather young."

"Don't you think that more is needed than just co-operation? Surely the most useful way would be if officers could recognize the kind of cases which would benefit by the kind of help you and your colleagues could give."

"That's true."

"If so, has the time not come when some formal teaching should take place, perhaps at a university department?"

"It would certainly be worthwhile to look into that."

"Perhaps you could start something in London, and who knows, tomorrow the rest of the country may follow suit. Tell me, John, what would be the main points you would emphasize if you were given a chance to teach our staff?"

This was not easy to answer and I thought for some minutes.

Then I said:

"It seems to me that hospital treatment may be an essential part of therapy, but that no permanent effective change will result unless we treat the patient and his family too. And this treatment of the patient and his family would perhaps have to be undertaken by more than one social worker. You see, Ron, if the treatment is given only in the hospital, and if it is patient-centered; and if by a combination of skill and good luck this patient is relieved of his symptoms or cured of his illness and returns to the community and his home, it is not unusual to find that some months later someone else, a wife, a child, or a mother breaks down. I have thought a lot about these things in the last few years. It seems to me that there are forces in family life which hitherto we have not investigated, and as mental illness occurs within the structure of the family, the whole family is in a sense a participant of the illness, in varying degrees."

"What fascinated me," Ron said, "was what you said some time ago about the effect of culture on mental health."

"Yes, I replied, "but the culture is not a static condition; it changes with time, and man needs constant adjustment to these changes. Some people can adapt themselves to it more than others. And some people cannot adapt at all. Did I tell you about that old lady I used to visit in Crouch End?'

"Yes, indeed you did."

"Perhaps you can see that she broke down for two reasons. First, because she was conditioned by her background to live a life of isolation; and secondly, because the world had changed and her way of life was forced to change with it."

"What I find most interesting in the Hendon Experiment," Ron said, "is how little of themselves people really show to us. And what they do show is often only part of the picture."

"That again is because of social conditioning."

"What do you mean?"

"I mean simply that people will play a certain role when they come to see you because they are conditioned to consider civil servants in that capacity only; and they do not imagine that a civil servant could be interested in them as people."

"That's true enough."

"The same thing applies to doctors. Nowadays people don't discuss their personal and work problems with their general practitioners as they used to in the old days."

"Of course not, because the doctor is so busy under the National Health Service."

"Quite. In the old days the family doctor was a kind of social worker too. Now we have split these professional functions. It is the same with National Assistance Board officers. As far as the applicant is concerned, they are there for one purpose only, to give him money, and accordingly they present to him that part of their personality connected with money. This is, I think, why the project between the Board and me gives a much more complete picture than we could achieve separately."

"That certainly was the case with Frank, wasn't it?"

"Yes, indeed. I remember clearly that he presented a completely different picture to you and to me, because his needs were different, as he thought, with each of us."

"Do you think, then, that a time will come when Ministry of Labor officers and National Assistance Board officers will have to be trained social workers?"

"I certainly do."

"Then the first step in that direction would be a kind of reorientation course. You must see about it, John."

* * *

Simultaneously with the Hendon Experiment, another experiment was being conducted to verify the first. This was done with the assistance of Fabian, a GP. (This, of course, is not his real name, as ethical reasons prevent me from giving it.) Fabian and I decided to see some of his patients together at his home, and for this we reserved one afternoon each week. He would tell me something about his patient's medical history, and then we tried to assess together his emotional problems. In this way I began to learn that the medical aspects of a case can be as important as the psychological, while Fabian learned that one cannot disregard the emotional aspects when looking for the underlying cause of symptoms. We asked ourselves, which was the chicken and which was the egg? A migraine had been regarded previously by Fabian as a simple "headache," for which he would produce various drugs to eliminate the symptom. But now he realized that the migraine was only the visible part of the iceberg, and that beyond it were serious problems which had to be dealt with. It also became clear to both of us that some patients presented their symptoms – or, to use Fabian's own words, "offered" their symptoms – as a means by which they begged for help for the causes which lay behind the symptoms. We learned as time went on that the symptom was a symbolic language, and that no change could take place by either reassurance or medicine, until we had picked up the underlying cause. Then it often happened that we succeeded in stopping the migraine, as well as the medicine. For me it was fascinating to learn how emotional problems manifested themselves in a physical area, and how a head, sinus, stomach or heart could be selected by disturbed emotions as a target area. It made me wonder not only if doctors needed more training in psychiatry, but if we social workers needed more training in medicine.

In this experiment with Fabian, we picked the same number of cases as in the Hendon Experiment. Fabian, after a year's work, assessed the result by concluding that much less medicine had been given to those people we had seen and that fifty percent of them functioned measurably better than before. The results here were almost identical with those of the Hendon Experiment, and one could also have measured the financial saving in terms of reduction of drugs. Fabian's foresight laid the foundation of future cooperation between psychiatric social workers and doctors; and his main contribution lay in the fact that he was willing to share his practice with a layman.

CHAPTER FIVE

At the request of Fabian, in the autumn of 1956 I went to see a woman who for the past twenty years had been unable to leave her home because of agoraphobia, a fear that held her to the imagined security of her house, in which she lived in Hendon with an aged father. At the same time, she felt herself a prisoner, bound to the house by invisible ties. Occasionally, the ambulance would come for her, and with a violent effort she would manage to get to the outpatient clinic, where she received psychotherapy. The doctor also kept her on drugs, which helped her at night, and without these tablets she could not have slept at all.

Joan had been told by the doctors that her fear of the streets and of the world was a fear of herself; that she was using her "prison" as a protection against a world where men desired women, because she was so much afraid of men. She knew that there was considerable truth in what she had been told, but this knowledge did not help her to overcome her phobia in any way. She was forty-five, rather thin, with blue eyes that at times were beautifully alive and expressive, but which were usually very sad.

By the time I entered the scene everything humanly possible had been tried out. She had even received treatment for a number of weeks as an inpatient in a hospital. While she was away from home she was a little better, and occasionally could go out of the hospital accompanied by another patient. As soon as she returned home, however, she was again a prisoner. She had secretly cried a great deal about his, but by now she had resigned herself to the fact that she might have to face the four walls of her room for the rest of her life.

Sitting there in her room on that dark autumn night I not only listened to her sad words, but also listened to what was going on within me. My own reactions to pain are as important as the words I hear. The longer I listened, the more I understood that Joan was indeed afraid of the outer world, not only because of the possibility of being desired by men, but because, like a child, she could not believe that outside her own four walls she could be loved or appreciated. Because she was afraid of not being loved, she had imprisoned herself in her house, where at least she could be sure of her father's love. I also became aware as I listened, that the love she talked about was not merely sexual love, but the indefinable love that is born in human beings, and which under favorable circumstances partakes of sexual desire. This woman, at the age of forty-five, not only believed that she could not be desired by men, but she believed also that she could not be wanted by anyone.

My heart went out towards this fellow sufferer, whose words reminded me of a long-forgotten winter night in my own childhood years. It was more than thirty years ago, when one day mother got ill. I came back from school to find her lying in the white bed, pale, with black rings under her eyes. I was exceedingly alarmed, for I had never seen her ill throughout my life.

"What's the matter, Mummy?" I asked, with a palpitating heart.

She looked up sadly from her pillows, and said quietly:

"I am very ill, Jancsi, very ill indeed."

"What's wrong with you, Mummy?" I felt a strange, painful excitement, almost akin to pleasure, coursing through my veins.

"The doctor thinks that I may have pernicious anemia. It's an illness in which the white blood corpuscles eat up the red ones. It's a very serious disease."

"Are you going to get better, Mummy?"

She smiled. "If God helps me, I shall get better. But we shall need His help."

That night before I went to sleep, I said the Shema, the ancient prayer of Israel, turning towards our invisible God. Then I said in Hungarian:

"God of Israel and of the Universe ... help Mummy to get better. Please forgive my naughtiness, and don't make her ill because I am a naughty boy."

All this came flooding back into my memory, almost as if it was conveying a message that I only half understood. What was this message from the past? What could it be?

I sat in silence, listening to her, and then it suddenly came to me.

"Tell me, please, when did your mother die?"

There was a short silence, then she said:

"My mother died when I was twelve years old."

"Who looked after you, after your mother's death?"

"Father."

The pictures from my own past were flooding in again.

After my mother died, father was heartbroken. I wanted to make up to him for his loss, and tried my best to be a good son. It was not easy, because I was going through the period of adolescence, when by the nature of things I should have rebelled. But somehow, somewhere I felt responsible for my mother's death. Although I was well on in my teens then, I felt like a small child who has to make up to his father for the wrongs he has committed. I did not go out for weeks, and I looked after father *as if I was now mother*. Then my sister took over and firmly ordered me out of the house, and once more I could start to live again. Was it possible, I now asked myself, that Joan too had taken over the role of her mother? Was this the message of my memories?

"Can you tell me more about your mother?" I asked.

She replied that she had been a very good mother, who had never even raised her voice. Joan had loved her with all her heart and both parents had lived very happily together, with never a quarrel. Joan had been spoilt, being the only child.

It all sounded too good to be true. I did not imagine that Joan was hiding the truth from me for conscious reasons, but I did think that this angelic picture of a mother who never lost her temper was not a true picture. It was Joan's need to see her as perfect, because in comparison she could then feel very imperfect. Had Joan, in fact, "married" her father, and then felt guilty as well as pleased about this turn of events? Or had she merely felt it her duty to look after the old man who had looked after her when young? All these were questions that could not yet be answered.

I changed the subject.

"Tell me, what do you do all day?"

She looked into the flames, and tears came to her eyes. That was sufficient. Yes, I had learned by then that one must listen not only to words.

Everything that is most beautiful and tragic, human or superhuman can never be conveyed in words. Words are inadequate for the expression of love. A sigh, a tear, an involuntary movement of the hands, can say more than any words, however well chosen. Does not true prayer lie in those rare moments of communication between Man and God when words are absent and only the heart speaks? I was now becoming aware not only of the thoughts and feelings of my patient expressed without words, but also of something more. If that God in whom I believe is beyond the expressible, is He not also to be found in the pain that cannot be expressed? Is His miraculous spirit not present in the silent communication of men? And if this is so, is He not imminent in the relationship between Joan and myself. Is it not possible that He directed my memories and thoughts towards a greater understanding, that I might become an instrument in His hands to lift up this suffering human being from the dust? Every tiny particle is capable of reflecting the light and the warmth of the sun.

These silent thoughts of mine were not expressed in words to the patient ... but does one not communicate without words? I believe that one does. Not only do patients communicate in this way to the therapist, but the therapist communicates like-wise to the patient. The words I use may be the words of scientific thought, but my unspoken feelings are firmly rooted in my faith in a Power that is greater than any of us.

* * *

I went to see Joan regularly once a week and we talked about everything under the sun. If I had understood her problem correctly, then my role was to be a bridge between her "prison" and "freedom." If I could convince her that she was needed and wanted in the "outer" world, she might be able to break her bonds and be free again. But I realized that this could not be done instantaneously, after twenty years of unhappiness. I was also aware that with Joan verbal "interpretations" and "explanations" would never be effective. Joan needed the sense of reassurance which could only come if I was a constant visitor.

By the spring of 1957 she was taking a much greater interest in the world outside. While before she would sit by the fire away from the window, I found her during these weeks of spring *looking out*. Sitting by the window, she would look at the people outside, as if she had *to see* before she made the first step. I did not press her.

But one day she asked me if I would take her by car to my new office (we had recently moved from North Finchley to Wood Green), and accordingly a week later I took her to Wood Green, where she met my secretary and some of my colleagues. Soon afterwards, she said to me:

"I wonder if I could be of any help to you. You told me that you are writing a book, and that you also write articles. Do you think I could learn to type?"

I said that I would certainly see what could be done. I obtained permission from the Council for her to use the spare typewriter, and from then on, she came to Wood Green every Tuesday. The Red Cross, who had always been so helpful to us, also loaned her a typewriter for her private use to enable her to practice at home. Later through a friend of mine I managed to acquire another machine, which has now become her own property.

One day in my office when both my secretary and I were rather harassed, I ran out of cigarettes. Joan was sitting by the typewriter, and I turned to her.

"I wonder if you would do me a favor. I have run out of cigarettes. There is a shop around the corner. Would you be good enough to get me some?"

I had completely forgotten that Joan had not left her home alone for more than twenty years. I was so overwhelmed with work, that for some strange reason it had completely skipped my mind.

Without a word, she took her coat and left the office.

My secretary looked at me in alarm.

"Do you realize, Mr. Heimler, what you have done? You have sent her out alone."

For a few minutes I was uncertain what to do. Should I rush after her? Should I let her be, and when she came back take the whole affair for granted? Should I specially thank her?

She was much longer than the occasion warranted, but after about fifteen minutes she reappeared. She gave me the cigarettes and then said, pointing to a small parcel: "I also did a bit of shopping." Her eyes were shining and her face was slightly flushed. I had never seen Joan so happy.

I said simply: "Thank you for getting my cigarettes."

Later, when I took her home in the car, she said:

"I was alarmed at first, but now I am so pleased I was able to do it. Perhaps from now on I shall be able to do more and more. God bless you for getting me to do it."

* * *

By the end of the year Joan could type with reasonable speed, and she was indeed helpful to me in typing some parts of my manuscript. Because she knew now that she was needed, she was beginning to overcome her long-standing difficulties step by step. She could now go home by herself from my office by public transport; she could go out by herself to the hairdresser, do a bit of shopping, and even go out to meet people. And in living this happier life, she could still be a loving daughter to her old father, who was convinced that a "miracle had happened." To show my appreciation of what she had done, and to remind her that she was never alone, I brought her a golden cross for Christmas, which she has worn ever since.

I hope that Joan will grow yet further, and that one day she will use her own painful experience to help others. I am sure that she can do it, because it is through pain that she has grown herself. And I am grateful to her for teaching me that one can communicate without words.

Joan is another proof that in Community Care the methods must be different from established methods and different for different individuals.

* * *

When I showed Joan the part of this book which concerned *her*, she said:

"It is all very true, but something is missing."

Surprised, I looked up.

"What is missing, Joan?"

"You don't seem to have expressed what all this *really* means to me; what going out means to me."

I thought for a few seconds, then I said to her:

"Could you tell me, so that I can include it in the book?"

She looked at me with those blue eyes of hers and said:

"Perhaps it would be better if I wrote a letter to you about it, so that you could put the letter into your book."

This is the letter which I received from Joan, dated January 23, 1962:

Dear Mr. Heimler,

Thank you for letting me see the part that you wrote about me under the name of Joan. My first reaction to it was, as I told you the other day, that you have not fully expressed what this ability of going out really means to me. You have no idea how terribly happy I was the first time that I was able to travel home on my own from your office. It is no exaggeration to say that I went home with wings on my feet feeling more alive than I have for years. On the bus going home I held that little gold cross that you gave me in my hand, not because I was frightened, but because I felt very much alive.

To be a part of the crowd once more was an exhilarating experience. I had almost forgotten how people behaved, what is ordinary and normal to them, and I almost felt that I had descended from another planet.

It is a wonderful feeling to be able to do my own shopping now without having to rely on somebody else to do it for me. I can also visit my doctor, instead of him always having to come to me as he has done during the past years. I have found a new inner strength, and I confess to you now that I overcame my fear of going out because initially I wanted to maintain contact with you and I was frightened that as you were so busy you might not be able to come to see me every week.

I also discovered a purpose in life by doing a small job of work at your office. This is no doubt the beginning, but I am so pleased because I see now that I have a future. To be useful seems very important to me now.

Yours sincerely,
Joan.

MY LIFE AFTER AUSCHWITZ

CHAPTER SIX

On March 27, 1958, on my thirty-sixth birthday, I finished writing my book *Night of the Mist*. That evening I read it to Lily from beginning to end with a feeling that a chapter of my life was now closed, and a new one about to begin. Although it was dawn when I finished reading, Lily asked me to read again the pages describing how, in the concentration camp of Buchenwald, in that inferno, I had found a new meaning to my life. I read:

> As long as I can remember I have never been anything but a second-class citizen of the land where I was born. Despite the fact that according to documents my ancestors were Hungarian Jews as far back as the seventeenth century, and many of them engaged in agriculture – an occupation supposed to be untypical of the Jews – I myself was always discriminated against on account of my origin, and often by people whose own descent as Hungarian was questionable. In the course of time this feeling became manifest in the form of an inferiority complex; and this sense of interiority was apparent in a desire to excel over others, to "show 'em," out of sheer spite, that I could rise above the ordinary level. I had never considered the motives behind the urge for self-expression, or the problem of creativity. If there is talent lurking inside one, does it materialize from the depth of the soul under certain circumstances only, or is it inherited from our ancestors and

does it find a channel for its expression under any circumstances whatsoever? The question is prompted by the fact that during my adolescence I wrote poems, the majority of which appeared in print. In fact, in the part of Western Hungary where we were living I used to be known as "Heimler, the poet." My first volume of poetry was published when I was seventeen, on the very day the war broke out; the second appeared in 1943.

I always felt that I had to be better than others; that I had to "show the world" that I was not merely not second-rate but even better than first-rate. I was convinced that I had to answer to the world; it was only in Buchenwald that I learnt that I had to answer, ultimately, to no one but myself.

It was in Buchenwald that I learned, from Jews, Christians, Moslems and pagans, from Englishmen, Serbs, Rumanians, Czechs, Frenchmen, Belgians, Dutch, Russians, Greeks, Albanians, Poles and Italians that I was only one more suffering insignificant man; that the tongue my mother taught me, and my Hungarian memories, and the traditions of my nation, were nothing but artificial barriers between myself and others. For essentially, as Mankind, we are one. A slap in the face hurts an Englishman as much as it does a German, a Hungarian or a Negro. The pain is the same; only our attitude to the pain differs, according to the culture pattern of the country and the individual. Our dreams, each dreamt in a different language, spell out the same dream in the language of Mankind: all of us want peace, security, a life free from fear. And, each in our own way, irrespective of differences of nationality or race, seek for the meaning – or meaninglessness – of life and death, believe in God or deny Him, cry for a woman on whose bosom we may rest our tormented head. I also learned that it is a fallacy that there are great nations and little nations: there are merely nations which occupy a large territory and others which have less land. Greatness and smallness can exist side by side in any nation, just as they do in the case of individuals. This in its turn taught me to understand the pointlessness of ambition for the sake of fame or success, because as I was I was neither worse nor better than others. During the long walks in Buchenwald with Niels or Louis, I learned to understand that it is only through the grace of God that I am not a murderer like Dr. Ekstein, only through His grace that I am not impotent, or in love with a prostitute, like Louis. I learned that within me, as in others, the murderer and the humanitarian exist side by side; the weak child with the voracious male. That I am not in any way superior, that I am not different from others, that I am but a link in the great chain, was among the greatest discoveries of my life. From then on I resolved to support those who fell, even as I had been supported. When someone was despicable, greedy and selfish, I remembered all the occasions when I, too, had been despicable, greedy and selfish. Buchenwald taught me to be tolerant of myself, and by that means tolerant of others.

MY LIFE AFTER AUSCHWITZ

It may be that I would have learned this without the lesson of Buchenwald. But I would have learned it much later – perhaps too late.'

Lily's eyes were shining. She said:

"I always knew that one day you would write something that comes from your heart. I am glad that you have completed this book. You have fulfilled a promise that you gave yourself many, many years ago. You are a writer."

*   *   *

The editor of the *Jewish Quarterly,* a literary magazine of high standard, heard from a friend that I had written a book and asked to see it. As a result, in the summer issue of the *Quarterly* he published a chapter from *Night of the Mist* under the title "Smoke by Day – Fire by Night." A few days later, one of the literary advisers of a well-known publishing firm (who was in Florence at the time) read the piece and wrote to me that he would be interested to see the book. As I was fortunately going to Florence myself during the summer of 1958, I wrote back that I would hand the manuscript to him personally.

Whenever I am away from England, however happy I may be, I have a strange sense of loss of security, as a small child has when he leaves his mother behind. I know this is not common to ordinary Englishmen, who carry England within themselves wherever they go. But it seems to me that when I am on the continent I am nearer to my past and all its painful associations.

My British passport is my only visible symbol of belonging somewhere: "Her Britannic Majesty's Principal Secretary of State for Foreign Affairs Requests and Requires in the Name of Her Majesty..." How many times have I read and re-read these words! Only someone like me, with a similar past, could understand that these are not superficial sentiments, but perhaps a sign of the social psychosis of our age.

From the Gare de Lyons to Milan my sleeper was shared by a young man in his early twenties, who was also going to Florence, after having seen the beauties of Paris. I thought he came from Switzerland. He was a student architect, and he was very much looking forward to seeing, as he put it, "the living miracle of architecture." He was a nice young man, with big brown eyes and an excellent sense of humor.

He was not quite alone, he said, on this journey. In another compartment there was a girl. He did not know the girl yet, but he was certain he would by the morning. We made a bet about it.

It was a hot night in July and neither of us could sleep. The young man spoke English quite fluently, and we talked about this and that until the ticket collector came and asked for our passports, so that we need not be disturbed in the middle of the night at the French-Italian border. As he handed his passport down from the upper bunk where he was lying I caught sight of a two-headed eagle. My traveling companion was not Swiss after all.

He carried on in his light vein of conversation, but the very things at which I had laughed a few moments before I now considered superficial vulgarity; and I felt angry with fate at having to share my compartment with a German.

Logically I knew that he was too young to have had any part of the hideous past, that he was a nice well-mannered lad, and yet I could not help feeling hostile and resentful towards him. I hated him because of his race, and I was ashamed of it. How could I of all people hate someone because of his race?

He must have noticed that I had changed, for after some little time he came down from his bunk and asked me what the matter was. He was serious now.

"Are you an Englishman?" he asked.
"I'm a British citizen," I said, and opened my manuscript.
"Were you born in Britain?"
"No."
"May I ask where you come from?"
"I was born in Hungary."
He sat there, and I pretended to read my book. The air was full of tension.
"Is that your book?"
"Yes, it is."
"Are you a writer?"
"Yes, I am."
"What is the book about?"
For a minute I hesitated, and then I said:
"It is a book about German concentration camps."
His face flushed. He stammered:
"Co-con-centration camps?"
"*Jawohl!*"

As soon as I had said it I was sorry. By using the German word I had tried to humiliate him. My desire to humiliate this young man was causing me to feel guilty, and yet at the same time I asked myself why I should feel hurt for wanting to hurt the German. Then it occurred to me that this was the argument of the SS; to hurt, to kill the Jew is not a sin; it is an act of delousing. The feelings I was experiencing were not my own feelings, but theirs. I felt confused. I was doing to him what they had done to me. I was persecuting an innocent man whose only sin was that he happened to be born in Germany.

"You are Jewish, aren't you?"
His words were whispered, almost an apology.
"I am."
"Is it really true, all that I have heard?"
I handed my manuscript to him. "Read this. It is all there."

MY LIFE AFTER AUSCHWITZ

* * *

In the morning he waited until I was dressed. Then he said:
"You must hate me very much."
I did not answer. He went on:
"I would hate you, if it were the other way round. May I tell you something?"
"Yes, do."
"I was seven years old when the war ended. I remember that spring. You must remember it, too. The snow lasted until May. It was very cold."
"Yes, I remember."
I was again aware that I resented this common memory. How does he dare to have the same memories about that fateful spring?
He went on:
"I remember when the Americans arrived. A few days before they came, the Führer's picture disappeared from the wall. You must remember that I was a child and was brought up to believe in the Führer, and to hate the Allies. But now they had arrived and I couldn't believe it. I thought it was a bad dream, that I would wake up and find everything as it had been, and that Germany would still win the war. When I was five or six, Herr Heimler, I had some tin soldiers. You must have had the same kind when you were a small boy. My German soldiers always won, but some of them were Jews, and I wanted the Jews to lose. Perhaps you can understand what defeat has meant to me. My father...." His voice had changed. "He was in the SS, and he disappeared after the war. He never returned, and I hated the Allies and the Jews for it. And now I have read your story about your feelings as a child, and I realize you hated us the same way as I hated you when I was a child."

When we arrived in Milan the German boy asked me whether he could join me for breakfast on the way to Florence, and I agreed. The train was racing across northern Italy. The sun was shining and the sky was cloudless. Everything seemed unreal and perfectly beautiful. How could I sit there with a German? How could I speak as if there were not a world between us?

"You don't say very much. Did they hurt you a lot?"

I nodded.

"I can see it is even difficult for you to speak to me. But insanity must stop somewhere."

At last I found words to reply.

"I know it is insane, and I am truly sorry. But you must realize that in you I see reflected everything that happened to me, although I know that you are not responsible. I would like to forgive you, but how can I, how can I forget what happened to my father, my sisters, my aunts, uncles, nephews and cousins, and my six million comrades who were destroyed? I want to forgive you, and yet something stops me. And yet I believe that you and I are both the victims of some terrible mistake."

As he drank his coffee I saw tears in his eyes. I wanted to reach out to him, but I could not and the moment passed. We sat there silently, for a long time.

How easy it is to hate, I said to myself, because hate is so much a human heritage. Is it not possible that behind my hate for the Germans, the Gestapo, the guards, there is a personal hate too that was there long, long before Hitler came on the scene?

My heart beat fast, and for a fleeting moment I saw a terrible picture that I tried to evade. It was the memory of a summer evening, and my father was angry with me; he hit me very hard and I cried out. I was small and he was big – and now, in one awful moment, I saw him in an SS uniform. Yes, it was that hate too that I had to overcome. One day, when I had been able to achieve it, perhaps I could reach out towards this young German again.

* * *

My uncle and cousins in Florence were Italian, and this was my first visit to them since the end of the war. My uncle in his young days used to live in Fiume. Fiume had been part of the Austro-Hungarian monarchy, but after the First World War the Treaty of Versailles had given it to Italy. My cousins could speak little Hungarian, but uncle still used the rich-flavored Hungarian words of a former age.

When I told my cousins that I was going to meet the literary adviser of a publishing company at the Piazza della Republica, they disappeared, so that I could "negotiate" in private. And there I sat, my manuscript under my arm, waiting for him.

It was a warm afternoon. The restaurant was in shadow, but a hot breeze blew from the direction of the Arno. The red umbrellas struck a cheerful note, and the chimes of the Dome mingled with jazz music. An Italian soprano was singing *"Volare ... oh ... oh ... Cantare ... oh, oh, oh oh!"*

I closed my eyes, and was back in our garden at home in Savaria. The chestnut trees were swaying in the wind of a summer night. My little friend Laci was talking to me about the future.

"And what will you be when you grow up, Jancsi?"

"I want to be a writer; you know, someone who writes books. A Jew can be a writer. After all, the Bible was written by Jews."

"That's true," said Laci seriously, "the Bible was written by Jews."

"Not all of it," I corrected myself. "Some parts were written by Gentiles."

"Still, the nice parts were written by Jews."

"And what about you, Laci? What do you want to be when you grow up?"

We must have been about ten years old. He pulled a face.

"Oh, I don't know. Mummy wants me to go into the business, but I'll tell you a secret. I want to be a pilot."

"Jews can't be pilots," I said, "but I think Jews can be businessmen."

"I will be a pilot all the same," said Laci, "even if I have to go to Palestine."

At this point Andrew joined us. He was two years younger than we were.

"It's easy for him," said Laci, pointing his finger at Andrew. "He can be whatever he likes. He's a Christian."

Andrew thought that Laci was saying something nasty about him. He protested:

"You shut up, you! I'm not a Christian! You're a Christian, and I shall be an electrical engineer."

At this point our mothers called us in for dinner. But before we went in Laci said:

"I'll make a bet with you that I shall be a pilot." He pushed his hand into mine. "Let's shake hands on it."

My dear, dear friend Laci, you lost that bet. You were killed in Buchenwald in the winter of 1944, and not even your ashes remain. But Andrew and I have fulfilled our early dreams. He survived the war, having fought for the Resistance against the Nazis, and has become an electronic engineer – and is still a Christian. And I, yes, I have become a writer.

I opened my eyes. Where is that man, why is he so late?

Then he was standing in front of me. That moment will remain with me as long as I live. It was the moment of fulfillment of all my childhood dreams.

* * *

MY LIFE AFTER AUSCHWITZ

Uncle Nicholas was six feet tall, had white hair, and at over eighty did not look more than sixty. He always walked very erect and very fast, considering his years. Every Sabbath morning, having emptied his pockets of even a handkerchief – for according to ancient law he was not allowed to carry anything on the day of rest – he would race down to the little synagogue behind the Dome; and also for religious reasons he could not think of taking a bus or a taxi.

Sometimes he would walk down to the "posh" synagogue, the big "cathedral" as he called it, where he complained that the service was impersonal and too far removed from the Eastern European tradition. In the "cathedral" the services were carried out according to Sephardi customs. The Sephardi Jews originated from Spain. Even the pronunciation of the Hebrew and the chanting of the ancient words were different. Uncle preferred the little old synagogue almost unknown to the traveler who seeks a place of worship in that beautiful city.

The "cathedral" was blown up during the war by the SS The mines were ready, the fuses were lit, but nothing happened. A number of SS men entered the synagogue to see what had gone wrong, and at the moment of their entry the explosion occurred, and they were buried under the ruins. Italians said that it was the anger of God that had sent them to their death.

Standing by my uncle's side and listening to the ancient chanting of the cantor, I thought of our little synagogue in Savaria, and I remembered father too. Uncle stood erect, then bowed before the mighty and invisible God of Israel, and as I looked at him he was indeed the image of my father. His movements, the lines on his face, the expression of his eyes, all seemed to bring back father from the grave. (Poor father, he never had a grave.) For a minute I felt as if the present were in the past and I was standing there beside my father, speaking to him.

"Father, I have had a glimpse of the future. I can see Florence, Italy, the little synagogue behind the Basilica. My dreams have come true. I am a writer, and my book may be published soon."

And father would have turned to me to say:

"Be quiet. You can tell me all about it when the service is over."

And then, on our way back home, he would have looked towards the distant hills and said:

"What did you say, Jancsi, about the future? Don't you know that everything that is, was, and always will be? Don't you know that yet, my son?"

Uncle Nicholas smiled at me and patted my shoulder. When the service was over and we were walking home he stopped in front of the Battistero di San Giovanni, and looked at the beautiful carvings of the bronze door.

"I can understand why we Jews have produced only a very small number of great sculptors."

"What do you mean, uncle?" I inquired, puzzled.

"*They* expressed the beauty of God in carvings, in statues, in buildings. But the spirit of God is missing from the pages of *their* history."

"I don't understand what you mean, uncle."

"A Christian looking at these beauties," he went on "might think that Christianity must have been a living force to have created all this splendor. But don't forget that the spirit of God must manifest itself in the life of the people, not only in paint and stone. At the very time these carvings were made, one of your ancestors, Isaac Abarbanel, arrived here in Florence from Spain, where he had been beaten and ridiculed by the Christians. What's the use of all the art of Florence if mankind remains untouched by the spirit of God?"

We walked slowly across the busy square, among the tourists taking photographs and the children feeding pigeons. A photographer darted in front of us and took a photograph of us both, but uncle and I went on with our conversation as if we had seen nothing.

"Is this not a general problem, uncle?" I asked. "Is it not that all men, irrespective of their religion, have been unable to recognize and accept that spirit that you talked about? Does this not equally apply to Jews, many of whom have remained Jews in name only, and instead of art have worshipped the Golden Calf?"

"There is one difference," he said. "Our leaders and teachers, even in our darkest hour, never preached hate; *their* leaders did."

"No, uncle, that is not true. The prophets and leaders of our people did at times speak in terms of hate against our enemies. The spiritual crisis is not confined to Christianity. It is a general problem of humanity. By recognizing these facts we may come to an understanding of each other at last, Jews and Christians alike."

"You may be right," he said thoughtfully. "We may have to start again from the very beginning. What will you yourself do about it?"

"I shall tell them that we have all failed equally. I shall tell them that it is essential to stand together. I shall tell them to forgive in order to be forgiven."

He smiled. "You talk like a Christian."

"No, uncle," I said. "I talk as a Jew."

EPILOGUE

In the spring of 1957, as a result of the Hendon Experiment, the first "Human Relations Course" for National Assistance Board Officers was initiated by the Extra Mural Department of London University, and I was appointed tutor and lecturer of that course. In the years following two courses were running concurrently under the aegis of the University, one for clerical and executive officers of the Board, and the other for National Assistance Board Managers; during the last year some Disablement Rehabilitation Officers of the Ministry of Labor also attended. Through all these lectures and seminars I have aimed at bringing home to my students the need for greater awareness of human problems and tolerance towards those who are unable to work.

Several provincial universities have also started these Human Relations Courses since 1958, and by now several hundred civil servants have taken this training.

During the summer of 1960 I was appointed as County Psychiatric Social Work Organizer to the Middlesex County Council (one of the first appointments of its kind) and I was able to participate in the shaping of our Mental Health Department in the light of the new Mental Health Act, 1959. Now the Human Relations Courses have been extended by the University to our Local Authority Social Workers and Health Visitors. We have also opened our doors to some Social Workers from other authorities, and thus I am involved in training courses catering for over 160 people. A number of eminent lecturers and tutors have joined our ranks, also my colleagues from the Middlesex County Council, and I am proud to be associated with them in this pioneer scheme of training.

Although this and other aspects of my work take up the major part of my time, I still have a few patients whom I see regularly. As the years go by they seem to be teaching me more and more, and at times I feel as if so far I had only scratched the surface of the problem of the mentally ill in the community.

THE END

About the Author

Eugene Heimler was born on March 27, 1922 in Szombathely, Hungary the son of a lawyer and prominent member of the social-democratic party. He became a successful poet in Hungary with two volumes of poetry published before he was twenty. At age 21 he was deported to Auschwitz and Buchenwald and survived with the help of his happy memories about his childhood and his beloved mother, who had died after a long illness shortly before the start of World War II.

His wife Eva, his father, sister and her little son were murdered in Auschwitz. In 1946 he married Lily, née Salgo and in 1947 Eugene and Lily immigrated to England. At Lily's untimely death (1984) she left two children, Susan and George.

Soon after he received his diploma as the first psychiatric social worker from Manchester University, he began to develop his own social-integrative method, which became well known in Europe, America and Canada under the name of *The Heimler Method of Social Functioning*.

Later on he returned to Germany in order to teach young Germans his unique approach in which frustration and suffering are used as potential for satisfaction and creativity, and as the means to find purpose and meaning in life. He became director of the Hounslow Project on Community Care (1965–71), consultant for the Ministry of Social Security in England, the World Health Organization, and the Government of the United States of America.

For 20 years he taught his subject at the University of London, England and his fame lead to chairs at several universities in the USA and Canada.

In 1985 Eugene Heimler received an honorary doctorate from the University of Calgary, Canada, where he had taught his subject for seventeen years.

On the day marking the 40th anniversary of the end of the war in Europe, he married Miriam Bracha with whom he spent the last, very happy and fulfilled years of his life. Dr. Heimler died on December 4th, 1990.

His work is being continued by practitioners, lecturers and researchers around the world.

When the Germans invaded Hungary in 1944, Eugene Heimler was twenty-one. His father, a socialist as well as a Jew, was arrested by the Gestapo and never seen again. Mr. Heimler and his new wife were taken from a Hungarian ghetto and deported in a cattle truck to Auschwitz. His wife and family died there, but he survived to be taken to Buchenwald and other camps in Germany. At the end of the European war, he escaped and found his way back to his native country. NIGHT OF THE MIST is an account of a young man's experience under the Gestapo. It records the day-to-day events, the miserable conditions of existence, the physical suffering endured by the prisoners. But Eugene Heimler goes beyond a factual record of events. With a gifted insight he describes the deeper effects of suffering – on their minds. He writes not only of himself but of many others imprisoned with him: of the doctor and the architect, no longer middle-class gentlemen of authority, but near animals; of the girl, once gentle and intelligent, now offering her diseased body for a crust of bread; of the man who spent twelve years in prison for the murder of his wife, and who in the inferno of a concentration camp found meaning in life.Yet, though he knew the worst of humanity, Heimler was able to regain his faith in God and in the dignity of man. He does not hate; and the horror of his experience is transcended by his compassion and deep understanding of spiritual values. The true message of his book is not one of horror, but of hope.

(*My Life After Auschwitz*)

In this second powerfully written volume of Eugene Heimler's incredible life's journey from a persecuted Jewish child in a small town in Hungary to world-renowned writer, therapist and teacher, Heimler is on his way home to Hungary from the concentration camps of Germany, where he had lost all his family. On this journey he experiences many life-threatening moments: being on a train with a former German SS man; witnessing the brutal rape of his traveling companion by Russian thugs; attempts on his life and being arrested and charged with treason in Hungary.

Eventually he reaches England and remarries, but his trials are manifold. After hearing that the Secret Police are torturing his friends in Budapest, he realizes he can never return to Hungary and has a breakdown. When psychoanalysis helps him come back to life and regain his hope for the future, he is ready to act on an early ambition to become a writer and psychologist. He starts to write Night of the Mist, which has become a world classic, and becomes a psychiatric social worker, eventually becoming the County Psychiatric Social Work Organizer for the Middlesex County Council. These challenges have their obstacles as well, and Heimler vividly describes his work as a psychiatric social worker, including his refusal to give up on others – and himself. His experiences eventually lead to the development of a new method of therapy, which is today known as the Heimler Method of Social Functioning.

Throughout his life, Heimler consistently fought to help victims gain the courage to become victors. In A Link in the Chain, also published as My Life After Auschwitz he once more tells his stories poetically and vividly.

After surviving the worst trauma in human history Eugene Heimler transformed his pain and suffering into a model of healing that illuminates secrets to learning how to thrive and overcome whatever obstacles are in your path.

In The Healing Echo Dr. Heimler teaches you his unique empowering self-help method – how to transform your frustration and destructive impulses into creativity and new opportunities for flourishing.

In his innovative approach he gives you tools to develop a more resilient way of dealing with the stresses in your life, to overcome problems and to find meaning and purpose.
In this book you can learn to help yourself by listening to your inner voice and thus hear your *healing echo*.

THE STORM

THE STORM is a powerful drama in verse that reveals the secret of the survival of the Jewish people and how the Jews have been able to overcome history's never-ending challenges.

The drama is rooted in the author's personal Nazi death-camp experiences and his ongoing meditation on the Jewish tragedy of Masada. It illuminates how societal barbarism enabled Romans, Christians and Nazis to avoid and deny personal responsibility for their hatred, cruelty and massacres. Yet, despite a history punctuated by atrocities, Heimler breathes hope into the future for Jews, by voicing God's affirmation of the eternity of their survival.

This masterpiece is particularly relevant today, as extremism, antisemitism and intolerance sweep like wild fire across university campuses as well as Western- and Middle Eastern societies. The timeless message of Dr. Heimler's deeply moving drama is needed now more than ever before, to penetrate souls and educate minds.

What began as a teenager's innocent, promising verse grew, through the nightmare of the Shoah, into a profound, mature human soul, plumbing the depths of history, philosophy and faith.

Rabbi Dr. André Ungar, New Jersey

Eugene Heimler is a true Jewish hero of the twentieth century.

Ronald A. Lewis, M.Ed.

MESSAGES
A Survivor's Letter to a Young German

Eugene Heimler, in his captivatingly poetic style, takes you with him on a life-transforming journey through seas of imagination and rivers of tears; from storms of pain to pools of individual and communal wisdom as well as deep inside his self and yours.

His universal and autobiographical stories, like the vivid colors on the canvas of a water-color artist, flow and dynamically blend time dimensions into an expanding, cohesive whole.

The diversity of genre, time and metaphor is startling and reveals multiple layers of our physical, emotional and spiritual reality.

The author transcends time as he interweaves past, present and future into a tapestry of deep meaning and passion, stained by blood and marked by tears and joy.

This book is about the author's journey of losing, searching and re-finding his own identity and place in his physical, emotional and spiritual worlds.

In his "stream of consciousness" musings Heimler crosses time from biblical through medieval to modern human experiences of transformation through pain to self-discovery.

This artful intimate intertwining of personal, particular and universal themes draws the reader into Heimler's awe-inspiring multi-layered world of courageous introspection.

Messages illuminates how Heimler, as a Holocaust survivor, struggles to re-discover meaning, purpose and passion from his once shattered world.

Working through these challenges leads him to existential questions about the very meaning of life:

What are the connections between life and what we call death?

How can meaning transcend suffering?

How can we find peace if we deny our worst hours?

How can we understand all the hatred that surrounds us?

How can hate be turned into creativity instead of self-destructiveness?

What can keep our love and our ability to love alive in the midst of atrocities or indifference?

Come, join this remarkable man in his quest for eternal wisdom!

Can one benefit from suffering, pain and frustration? Prof. Dr. Eugene Heimler claims that, what we experience as frustration, is our potential for satisfaction. Based on his method of Social Functioning we can transform our weakness and what we call 'negative' into strength and to our own satisfaction as well as to the benefit of society. A certain amount of frustration serves as a driving force in our lives, that we need in order to be creative.

In this book, using case studies, Heimler describes how we can create a balance of satisfaction and frustration by means of the use of his method of Social Functioning and of the Heimler Scale, by observing and listening to ourselves.

Eugene Heimler's self-help-method of Social Functioning was developed and tested and proved extraordinarily successful.

In Constructive Use of Destructive Forces also published as Survival in Society Heimler describes in detail his interviewing and therapy techniques with individuals, couples and groups. His goal is to help them use their inner resources and past experiences.

The Heimler Method is applied with those needing therapy as well as 'healthy' individuals who want to explore their unused potential; it is used by teachers to help students become more creative; in the relationship between employers and employees; as well as by social workers and other helping professions.

NAPFOGYATKOZÁS UTÁN

A Nyugat-magyarországi Szombathelyen született, boldog családban nőtt fel. Szülőhazájának kedves tája és kultúrája, valamint a zsidó szellemi örökségéhez való szenvedélyes kötődés vette körül. 17 éves korában jelent meg első verseskötete: az ártatlanság, a gyengédség és a csodálatos ígéret versei.

"…Mikor még gyerek voltam anyám azt akarta, hogy költő legyek. Egy téli estén az ölében ültem s megvallotta, hogy ez a titkos vágya…"

Daughter of Abraham

For anyone on a life journey through pain towards transformation, Miriam Bracha Heimler's intimate, powerful memoir will help deepen your determination to overcome life's seemingly insurmountable obstacles.

Through touching vignettes Heimler paints vivid portraits of her continuing life challenges:

She escapes Communist East Germany as an 11 year old just before the rise of the Berlin Wall, leaving her Nazi father behind.

Despite her manifold struggles to overcome loneliness and poverty in her strange new world, and in defiance of having to fight peers' prejudice and feelings of inadequacy, she succeeds.

She makes many growth-steps on her way through the gates of her spiritual development.

Heimler's endearing, earthy, captivating style draws the reader into her multi-layered inner world of imagination, determination and hope.

The depth of the scenes she paints is reminiscent of great literature of the past, rather than superficial current works. The reader will enrich her / his life by diving into this real life treasure of vulnerability.

www.ingramcontent.com/pod-product-compliance
Lightning Source LLC
Chambersburg PA
CBHW031347040426
42444CB00005B/213